BRIGHT NOTES

HARD TIMES
BY
CHARLES DICKENS

Intelligent Education

IP INFLUENCE PUBLISHERS

Nashville, Tennessee

BRIGHT NOTES: Hard Times
www.BrightNotes.com

No part of this publication may be used or reproduced in any manner whatsoever without written permission, except in the case of brief quotations in critical articles and reviews. For permissions, contact Influence Publishers http://www.influencepublishers.com.

ISBN: 978-1-645420-56-9 (Paperback)
ISBN: 978-1-645420-57-6 (eBook)

Published in accordance with the U.S. Copyright Office Orphan Works and Mass Digitization report of the register of copyrights, June 2015.

Originally published by Monarch Press.
Paul M. Ochojski, 1966
2019 Edition published by Influence Publishers.

Interior design by Lapiz Digital Services. Cover Design by Thinkpen Designs.

Printed in the United States of America.

Library of Congress Cataloging-in-Publication Data forthcoming.
Names: Intelligent Education
Title: BRIGHT NOTES: Hard Times
Subject: STU004000 STUDY AIDS / Book Notes

CONTENTS

1) Introduction to Charles Dickens — 1

2) Introduction to Hard Times — 11

3) Textual Analysis
   - Book 1: Sowing, Chapters 1–8 — 18
   - Book 1: Sowing, Chapters 9–16 — 38
   - Book 2: Reaping, Chapters 1–6 — 55
   - Book 2: Reaping, Chapters 7–12 — 72
   - Book 3: Garnering — 85

4) Character Analyses — 105

5) Critical Commentary — 112

6) Essay Questions and Answers — 120

7) Bibliography and Guide to Further Research — 126

INTRODUCTION TO CHARLES DICKENS

EARLY LIFE

Charles Dickens was born on February 7, 1812, in Portsea. His father, John Dickens, was a minor clerk in the Navy Pay Office; his father's parents had been servants and his mother's parents only slightly higher on the social scale. John Dickens was a happy-go-lucky, improvident man whose family often knew want as the debts piled up. At the age of twelve, Charles Dickens experienced what was to become the key event of his life. His father was imprisoned for debt in the Marshalsea Prison; young Charles was taken out of school and put to work in a blacking warehouse in London, pasting labels on bottles of shoe polish. Although he later returned to school for a time, this experience left a permanent mark on the soul of Charles Dickens. Even many years later, after he had become a successful author, he could not bear to talk about it, or be reminded of his family's ignominy.

At the age of fifteen Dickens began working as an office boy for a law firm. He taught himself shorthand and by 1828 he became a reporter for the lay courts of *Doctors' Common*. The dull routine of the legal profession never interested him, so he became a newspaper reporter for the *Mirror of Parliament*, *The True Sun*, and finally for the *Morning Chronicle*. (John Forster, later his closest friend and biographer, was also employed at *The True Sun*.) By the age of twenty, Dickens was one of the best Parliamentary reporters in all England.

During this same period Dickens' interest began to switch from journalism to literature. His first work of fiction, "Dinner at Poplar Walk" (later reprinted as "Mr. Minns and His Cousin"), appeared in the *Monthly Magazine* when he was twenty-one. His newspaper work had given him an intimate knowledge of the streets and byways of London, and late in 1832 he began writing sketches and stories of London life. They began to appear in periodicals and newspapers in 1833, and in 1836 were gathered together as *Sketches by Boz, Illustrations of Every-day Life, and Every-day People*. This pseudonym, Boz, was suggested by his brother's pronunciation of "Moses" when he had a cold.

PICKWICK PAPERS

The success of the *Sketches* brought an invitation from the publishers Chapman and Hall in 1836 to furnish the "letter-press" for a series of cartoon sketches about a humorous cockney sporting club. (The letter-press was little more than a running accompaniment, like an ornamental border around the drawings.) The project had hardly begun when Robert Seymour, the artist, committed suicide. Dickens searched long for a new artist and found an ideal collaborator in H. K. Browne ("Phiz"), but Dickens had persuaded the publisher to let him improvise a fictional narrative. When the *Posthumous Papers of the Pickwick Club* finally came out, the story predominated over the illustrations.

When *Pickwick Papers* appeared in April, 1836, as a monthly serial, the sales were at first discouraging. Of the first issue, a modest 400 copies were printed; later the work became increasingly popular. Some 40,000 copies of each issue were sold. After the last installment appeared in November, 1837, the novel was published in book form. This set the pattern for all of Dickens' subsequent novels.

The success of *Pickwick* convinced Dickens that his real career lay in writing fiction; he gave up his Parliamentary reporting in order to devote himself full time to it. In 1836 he had married Catherine Hogarth, the daughter of one of the owners of the *Morning Chronicle*; his growing family made it necessary to work exhaustingly at his writing. His next work, *Oliver Twist*, began appearing even before *Pickwick* was completed. *Nicholas Nickleby* followed in a like manner in 1838–39, and the very first number sold some 50,000 copies. During this same period he was editor of Bentley's Miscellany (1837–39). By the 1840s Dickens had become the most popular novelist in Britain, taking over the place long held by Sir Walter Scott.

THE MIDDLE YEARS

The years between 1840 and 1855 were most fruitful ones: *The Old Curiosity Shop, Barnaby Rudge, A Christmas Carol, Martin Chuzzlewit, Dombey and Son, David Copperfield, Bleak House, Little Dorritt*, and *Hard Times* all appeared. In addition, he made his first trip to America; copyright laws at that time allowed American publishers to pirate his works, and their lack of concern over this injustice undoubtedly contributed to Dickens' unfavorable criticism of America in *Martin Chuzzlewit*. In 1850 Dickens founded his own periodical, *Household Words*, and continued to edit it until he and his partner exchanged it for *All the Year Round* in 1859. *Hard Times, A Tale of Two Cities*, and *Great Expectations* appeared in serial form in these publications. But these years of literary success were marred by domestic strife. He and his wife had never been particularly suited to each other, and their marriage ended in separation in 1856.

In addition to writing, Dickens had another love - amateur theatricals - which led him into yet another pursuit in the latter part of his career. He gave public readings from his novels from 1859 to 1868 in England, Scotland, and America. He had always loved the theater - he studied drama as a young man and had organized an amateur theatrical company of his own in 1847 (he was both manager and principal actor).

His energies never seemed to fail: he burned the candle at both ends. He published *Our Mutual Friend* in 1864–65 and at his death left an unfinished novel, *The Mystery of Edwin Drood*, a suspense tale in the nature of a detective story. He died suddenly in 1870 from a stroke at the age of fifty-eight. G. K. Chesterton once said that Dickens died of "popularity." It would seem so; his exhaustive burden (marked by insomnia and fatigue) is well cataloged in his letters. He was buried in the Poets' Corner of Westminster Abbey.

Dickens wrote with an eye on the tastes of a wide readership, never far ahead of the printer, and was always ready to modify the story to suit his readers. For example, when the sales of serial installments of *Martin Chuzzlewit* fell from 60,000 to 20,000, Dickens sent his hero off to America in order to stimulate renewed interest. No novelist ever had so close a relationship with his public, a public ranging from barely literate factory girls to wealthy dowagers, but consisting mostly of the newly formed middle classes.

TEACHER AND ENTERTAINER

Walter Allen in *The English Novel* points out that Dickens became the spokesman for this rising middle class, and also its teacher. "Dickens more than any of his contemporaries was the expression of the conscience-untutored, baffled, muddled as it doubtless often was-of his age," he writes. Not only in his novels, but in his magazine, *Household Words*, Dickens lashed out at what he considered the worst social abuses of his time: imprisonment for debt, the ferocious penal code, the unsanitary slums which bred criminals, child labor, the widespread mistreatment of children, the unsafe machinery in factories, and the hideous schools.

Yet, as Allen suggests, Dickens was primarily a great entertainer, "the greatest entertainer, probably, in the history of fiction." It is significant that Dickens was not satisfied to have his books the best sellers of their time. He wanted to see his audience, to manipulate it with the power of his own words. His public readings gave him an excellent opportunity to do so. Sitting alone on a bare stage, he would read excerpts from various novels, act them out really, imitating the voices of the various characters. These theatrical readings would always contain a dying-child scene or two which left his audience limp and tear-stained. Dickens suffered all the emotions with his audience, even after repeated readings, and this undoubtedly helped to shorten his life. He entertained his readers with humor, pathos, suspense, and melodrama, all on a grand scale. Charles Dickens had a fertile imagination that peopled his novels with characters and events which continue to entertain twentieth-century readers as they delighted his contemporaries.

NOVEL TECHNIQUE

An understanding of Dickens as an artist requires an understanding of the method of publication he used-monthly or weekly installments. Serialization left its mark on his fiction and often accounts for the flaws which many critics have found in his work. John Butt and Kathleen Tillotson in *Dickens at Work* (1957) describe the problems serial publication imposed:

"Chapters must be balanced within a number in respect both of length and of effect. Each number must lead, if not to a **climax**, at least to a point of rest; and the rest between numbers is necessarily more extended than what the mere chapter divisions provide. The writer had also to bear in mind that his readers were constantly interrupted for prolonged periods, and that he must take this into account in his characterizations and, to some extent, in his plotting."

This technique brought on a loose, episodic treatment with a vast, intricate plot, numerous characters and much repetition to jog the reader's memory. Instead of the whole novel slowly building to a real **climax**, each part had to have a little **climax** of its own. In *Hard Times* the bad effects of serialization are at a minimum because it is a comparatively short novel (about 260 pages in most editions) and it appeared in weekly rather than monthly parts. But the careful reader can still tell where each part ended; considerations of space rather than of artistic technique formed the story.

The works of Dickens have many of their roots in the eighteenth century, especially in the novels of Tobias Smollett, whom he greatly admired. From Smollett he borrowed many devices of characterization - "tagging" characters with physical peculiarities, speech mannerisms, compulsive gestures, and eccentric names. Examples in *Hard Times* include the distinctive speech pattern of Stephen Blackpool, who talks in a phonetically transcribed Lancashire dialect; the self-deprecating speech of Bounderby or the self-pitying talk of Mrs. Sparsit; the physical peculiarities of Bitzer, the epitome of pallidness; the names of characters - Bounderby, M'Choakumchild, Gradgrind-so evocative of their personalities.

The eighteenth century also brought the picaresque tradition in fiction to full flower. (The term refers to novels which depict the life of a picaro [Spanish: "rogue"] and which consist of unconnected **episodes** held together by the presence of the central character.) Early novels, especially those of Defoe, Fielding, and Smollett, were rambling, episodic, and anecdotal. Many of the novels of Dickens-*Pickwick*, *Oliver Twist*, *David Copperfield* - to name a few - are picaresque in technique. *Hard Times* borrows from the tradition only the irreverent, satirical view of stuffed-shirt pretentiousness and of established society in general. The eighteenth-century theater, with its sharply defined villains, its involved melodramatic plots, and its farcical humor, also suggested ideas for plots and characterizations to Dickens.

Dickens took his descriptive techniques from Sir Walter Scott and other early nineteenth-century novelists. No character, no matter how minor, appears on the scene without being fully described, not only as to physical appearance, but as to the clothing he wears. Dickens also excels in the short but evocative description of places; in *Hard Times* note the portrayal of the murky streets and factories of Coketown and of its blighted wasteland-like countryside.

THE WORLD OF HIS NOVELS

The world of Dickens' novels is a fantasy world, a fairy-tale world, a nightmare world. It is a world seen as through the eyes of a child: the shadows are blacker, the fog denser, the houses higher, the midnight streets emptier and more terrifying than in reality. To a child, inanimate objects have lives of their own: thus the smoke malevolently winds over Coketown like serpents and the pistons of the steam engines in the factory are "melancholy mad elephants."

The characters, too, are seen as children see people. Their peculiarities are heightened to eccentricities; their vices, to monstrous proportions. Most of the people in his novels are caricatures, characterized by their externals, almost totally predictable in behavior. We know little about them beyond their surface behavior; Dickens focuses on the outward man, not the inner motives. It is interesting to note, however, that Dickens was able to create intensely individual portraits even though he lacked the ability to analyze motivation and character developments. His characters are more than types or mere abstract representations of virtue or vice. They are intensely alive and thus memorable. The characters from a Dickens novel are remembered long after the plots and even the titles of the books have been forgotten.

DICKENS THE REFORMER

Dickens in his lifetime saw Great Britain change from a rural, agricultural "Merrie Old England" of inns, stagecoaches, and fox-hunting squires to an urbanized, commercial-industrial land of railroads, factories, slums, and a city proletariat. These changes are chronicled in his novels, and it is possible to read them as a social history of England. *Pickwick*, although set in 1827–28, reflects much of what still survived of the old eighteenth-century way of life. *Oliver Twist* (1837–39) shows the first impact of the Industrial Revolution - the poverty existing at that time and the feeble attempt to remedy it by workhouses. *Dombey and Son* (1846–48) describes the coming of the railroad, a symbol of change. Dombey, the merchant, sacrifices love, wife, and children for a position of power through money; yet he is already obsolete, for the industrialist is the ruler now.

Dickens grew increasingly bitter with each novel; his criticism of society became more radical, his **satire** more biting and less sweetened by humor. In his later novels he often broke out in indignant exasperation and almost hysterical anger. He figuratively mounted a soapbox, demanding that the "Lords and Gentlemen" do something about the appalling conditions of the poor.

In his early novels, society itself is not evil; it is only some people who are bad and who create misery for others by their callousness and neglect. By the time of *Dombey and Son* it is institutions which are evil, representing in that novel the self-expanding power of accumulated money. *Bleak House* (1852–53) attacks the law's delay and the self-perpetuating mass of futility it has become. *Hard Times* (1854) savagely lampoons the economic theories which Dickens considered responsible for much of human misery. The English historian, Lord Macaulay, charged that it was full of "sullen Socialism." Of *Little Dorritt* (1855–57), which attacks prisons and imprisonment for debt, George Bernard Shaw said that it was "more seditious than Karl Marx." In *Our Mutual Friend* (1864–65) we see the fully disillusioned Dickens. The atmosphere of the novel is grim, permeated with a sense of growing nightmare. There is the feeling that something deep and basic is wrong with the social order, something beyond the mere reforming of bad people or poorly-run institutions.

    T. A. Jackson in *Charles Dickens: The Progress of a Radical* tries to claim him for the Marxists as a champion of the downtrodden masses. Yet Lenin, the father of Communist Russia, found Dickens intolerable in his "middle class sentimentality." George Orwell was probably correct when he stated that Dickens' criticism of society was neither political nor economic, but moral. Certainly Dickens offered no substitutes for the system or institutions he attacked. Thus in *A Tale of Two Cities* (1859) he expressed his loathing for the decadent French aristocracy of the ancient regime, but he seemed to like the triumphant democracy of the Revolution no better. In *Hard Times* he excoriates the exploitation of the industrial workers by the factory owners, but he is repelled almost equally by the attempt of the workers to form unions in self-defense. He seems to suggest that the Golden Rule is the only solution to class struggle.

HARD TIMES

INTRODUCTION

THE PLACE OF HARD TIMES AMONG THE NOVELS

As Edgar Johnson points out in *Charles Dickens: His Tragedy and Triumph* (II, 801), "*Hard Times* brings to a culmination an orderly development of social analysis that extends in Dickens' work from *Dombey and Son* through *Bleak House*." In the earlier novels he had touched upon "the rotten workings of the social system in almost every major institution and activity of society," except for mechanized industry which Dickens saw as "an inhuman, life-denying tyranny." *Hard Times*, rather than giving a detailed picture of industrial working activities, is "an analysis and a condemnation of the ethos of industrialism," according to Johnson.

Hard Times has never enjoyed the popularity of the uproariously funny *Pickwick Papers* or the autobiographical *David Copperfield*, nor has it been much esteemed by critics except in recent years. It is really a compact model of a typical Dickens novel: about one-third as long, with fewer characters to focus upon, fewer subplots to complicate things unnecessarily, more unity of **theme**, purpose, and action. Perhaps the reason is that Dickens wrote its 100,000-plus words in about five months, instead of allowing himself the twenty-month period he took for most novels. Its tone is grim, its structure tightly knit, its purpose serious; it remains an excellent example of Dickens' capability as a serious novelist. F. R. Leavis in *The Great Tradition* admits Dickens to his very exclusive circle of the great English novelists-Jane Austen, George Eliot, Henry James, and Joseph Conrad-on the strength of *Hard Times* alone. He writes that "of all of Dickens' works it is the one that has all the strength of his genius, together with a strength no other of them can show-that of a completely serious work of art."

BRIEF SUMMARY

The novel opens in a schoolroom where Mr. Gradgrind and the teacher, Mr. M'Choakumchild, are showing the pupils off to a visiting school inspector. Gradgrind is proud that in his school only facts are taught. He calls upon a girl, Sissy Jupe, to define a horse. Although her father is employed by the Horseriding, a sort of circus, she cannot do it in a factual way, and Bitzer, a boy, is called next. He gives the acceptable scientific definition.

On the way home Gradgrind catches two of his own children, Tom and Louisa, peeping in at the circus. He is dismayed that they, who have collections of seashells, minerals, and other factual objects at home, should be tempted by the silly circus world of fanciful imagination. When he arrives home with his culprits, he finds Mr. Bounderby, a banker and wealthy mill-owner there. Bounderby suggests that the bad influence of Sissy, the circus girl, is dangerously perverting his fact-trained children. They decide to call upon Sissy's father and have him remove the girl from the school.

As the men walk to their destination, Dickens describes Coketown, a grim and grimy industrial city, which provides no healthy outlets for its working population. They find Sissy but not her father. The circus people tell them that Jupe, a brokendown clown on the skids, has apparently deserted his daughter. Against the advice of Bounderby, Gradgrind, struck with compassion, agrees to take Sissy into his household and continue her education.

Sissy lives with the Gradgrinds, but is not changed by it. In fact she seems to be affecting Tom and Louisa, especially the latter. Tom is becoming a selfish lad who is looking forward to working in Bounderby's bank so as to escape the oppressive atmosphere at home. He urges Louisa to be pleasant to Bounderby in order to make things easier for him. As Tom is the only one she really loves, she is willing to do anything to please him.

Dickens next focuses our attention on Stephen Blackpool, a worker in Bounderby's textile mill, a sober, industrious, and long-suffering man. He is married to an alcoholic derelict who has left him, and is in love with Rachael, a fellow worker of angelic nature. When his drunken wife returns one night, the desperate Stephen goes to Bounderby to seek advice. He wants to know if it is possible for him to get a divorce. He is told that only the wealthy can do this by an Act of Parliament, a very expensive procedure. Stephen is in despair at the news.

When he returns to his rooms, he finds Rachael tending his ill wife. During the night the wife almost drinks a bottle of poison, but Rachael stops her while Stephen, paralyzed with hesitation, looks on. Yet he is grateful, even though his wife's death would have freed him.

Gradgrind becomes a Member of Parliament and goes off to London. Before he leaves he tells Louisa that Bounderby wants to marry her. She does not love him, but her reluctance is overcome by her father's statistics and hard-facts philosophy. Although she is prostituting herself by this marriage, she does it because Tom wishes it. She is estranged from Sissy, feeling ashamed for her easy surrender.

Bounderby breaks the news of his marriage to Mrs. Sparsit, his housekeeper, a widow formerly of high social position. She feels only pity for him for marrying a girl less than half his age. Mrs. Sparsit moves into an apartment over the Bank, where she is assisted by Bitzer, now an employee there. Tom, who now also works in Bounderby's bank, is described by Bitzer as a dissipated idler who is protected by his sister's position as Bounderby's wife.

Mr. James Harthouse, an effete gentleman, comes to Coketown on political business. He is attracted to Louisa, who is so different from the society girls he has known. She is attracted to him because he is so unlike her brassy, vulgar husband Tom Gradgrind is much impressed by Harthouse and attaches himself to him. He soon supplies Harthouse with the information about the domestic affairs of the Bounderbys which enables him to worm his way into Louisa's confidence.

Meanwhile Stephen Blackpool has refused to join the newly formed labor union because of a promise he made to Rachael. He is ostracized by his fellow workers after being denounced as a traitor to his class by Slackbridge, the union organizer. Stephen is called to Bounderby, who questions him about the union affair. Stephen, although ostracized, defends the rights of the workers and as a consequence is fired and blacklisted by Bounderby.

HARD TIMES

Stephen realizes he must seek work away from Coketown. He is with Rachael and an old woman whom he had met before outside Bounderby's house when Louisa and Tom come to visit. Louisa, sorry for Stephen, offers him money to tide him over. Tom, taking Stephen aside, tells him to wait outside the Bank at night for a message about a new job. Stephen does so, but when no one appears, he leaves Coketown to seek employment elsewhere.

Tom seems to be in financial troubles, which Louisa from time to time alleviates. When Harthouse promises to take Tom under his wing, he ingratiates himself with Louisa at last. He offers to lend Tom money, but Tom tells him he no longer needs it.

The next day the news breaks that the Bank has been robbed by someone entering it with a false key. Stephen Blackpool, having been seen loitering at night by Mrs. Sparsit and Bitzer, is the prime suspect. The old woman is supposed to be his accomplice.

Louisa suspects her brother of complicity, but when she asks him to confide in her, he has nothing to say. He asks her only not to tell of their meeting with Stephen, Rachael, and the old woman.

Mrs. Sparsit, who has been staying at the Bounderbys' after the robbery, precipitates a crisis between Bounderby and Louisa by her show of pity for him and hints that Louisa is not solicitous enough of his wants. Mrs. Sparsit watches Louisa and Harthouse growing closer together as a result, and she hopes to be able to reveal them as lovers to Bounderby.

When Bounderby goes on a business trip, Mrs. Sparsit sets a trap by telling Louisa she will not come out to see her. She sneaks out there nevertheless and eavesdrops on the supposed lovers in the garden. She overhears Harthouse declaring his love for Louisa and thinks they are arranging to elope. Later she follows Louisa to the railroad station, but loses her at her arrival in town.

Louisa, fleeing the unwelcome advances of Harthouse, has actually returned to her father's house. She reproaches him for the ruin of her life, and he admits that his philosophy has failed. She is entrusted to the care of Sissy, whose sunny presence has already transformed the other Gradgrind children.

Harthouse is visited by Sissy, who appeals to the lingering spark of decency in him, and he agrees to give up Louisa and leave Coketown. Bounderby is visited in London by Mrs. Sparsit, who tells him of the supposed elopement. He rushes to Gradgrind to confront him with his daughter's perfidy, and is surprised to find that Louisa is there. Gradgrind suggests that in their present strained relations, it would be best for Louisa to stay apart from him for a while. Bounderby lays down the ultimatum that if she doesn't return now, the separation is permanent.

Bounderby resumes his bachelor life, with Mrs. Sparsit as his housekeeper. He posts the town with placards offering a reward for the capture of Stephen Blackpool. Rachael, in order to help Stephen, tells Bounderby about the meeting with Tom and Louisa. She also says that Stephen has been notified and will return within two days to clear his name.

Days pass but Stephen does not appear, although he has left his new residence. He has simply vanished. Rachael is afraid that he has been murdered to shield the 'real criminal. Mrs. Sparsit, in the meantime, has been hunting the supposed accomplice of Stephen, the old woman known as Mrs. Pegler. Catching her, she brings her to Bounderby, only to discover that the old woman is really Bounderby's disowned mother. The rich braggart's reputation as a rags-to-riches self-made man is destroyed by this revelation.

Rachael and Sissy walking in the country find Stephen's hat at the brink of an abandoned mine shaft. When men come to investigate, they find Stephen at the bottom, still alive. He had fallen in on the way back to give himself up. Before he dies, he tells about Tom's request that he loiter at the Bank. But before Tom can be questioned, he disappears.

Gradgrind and Louisa are convinced now that Tom was the thief. It turns out that Sissy has arranged that Tom be hidden with Sleary's Horseriding until he can be spirited out of the country. They all go there, talk to him, but just as he is about to leave, Bitzer arrives to take Tom into custody. Bitzer refuses all appeals for mercy from Gradgrind, insisting that self-interest dictates that Tom be delivered over to justice. By a ruse, the circus master manages to get Tom to escape anyway.

Mr. Bounderby fires Mrs. Sparsit for her meddling, which has ruined his marriage and reputation. She in turn reveals her scorn for him. The novel ends with everyone having lost someone or something. Only the circus goes on, useless according to utilitarian standards, but giving people the joy and imagination which make life in the industrialized world bearable.

HARD TIMES

TEXTUAL ANALYSIS

BOOK 1: SOWING, CHAPTERS 1-8

CHAPTER 1: THE ONE THING NEEDFUL

"Now, what I want is, Facts. Teach these boys and girls nothing but Facts. Facts alone are wanted in life. Plant nothing else, and root out everything else. You can only form the minds of reasoning animals on Facts: nothing else will ever be of service to them. This is the principle on which I bring up my own children, and this is the principle on which I bring up these children. Stick to Facts, sir!"

The speaker is a man with "a wide, thin, and hard set" mouth, eyes like "two dark caves, overshadowed" by the "square wall of his forehead." His voice is "inflexible, dry, and dictatorial" and he emphasizes his remarks with "a square forefinger." His air is obstinate; his coat, legs, and shoulders are square; his very neckcloth seems to hold his throat "like a stubborn fact."

The scene is "a plain, bare, monotonous vault of a schoolroom," and the speaker, accompanied by the schoolteacher and another man, looks down upon the "inclined plane of the little vessels" - the pupils - arrayed before them "to have the facts poured into them until they were full to the brim."

Comment

The opening paragraph sets the tone of the entire book. Facts alone are needed. "Plant nothing else, and root out everything else," proclaims the speaker before we even know who he is. The planting, not only of "facts" but of the very way of life they represent, the utilitarian, is the theme of Book 1; thus its title, "Sowing."

To strengthen the atmosphere of factualism everything in the opening scene is bare, austere, and square. The speaker's forefinger, forehead, coat, legs, and shoulders are described as square. He is the epitome of "squareness" in the sense of the square being a figure of geometric exactitude.

CHAPTER 2: MURDERING THE INNOCENTS

The man of facts is Thomas Gradgrind, a man always ready "to weigh and measure any parcel of human nature, and tell you exactly what it comes to." No nonsensical beliefs could ever enter his head. Everything "is a mere question of figures, a case of simple arithmetic."

Comment

Dickens often gives his characters names that "tag" them symbolically. Gradgrind is one such name. Suggesting such things as grading, gradual, graduating and grinding, it expresses his chief characteristics.

Gradgrind faces the schoolchildren like a "cannon loaded to the muzzle with facts, and prepared to blow them clean out of the regions of childhood at one discharge. He seemed a galvanizing apparatus, too, charged with a grim mechanical substitute for the tender young imaginations that were to be stormed away."

Comment

The twin **metaphors** applied to Gradgrind - the cannon and the electrical galvanizing apparatus-reinforce Dickens' image of him as a mechanical man. He is the spirit of technology, of engines and of science, opposed to childhood and imagination because they are unproductive. This opposition of forces is the **theme** of the novel, and its plot demonstrates the result of Gradgrindism in action.

He calls upon "girl number twenty," who gives her name as Sissy Jupe. "Sissy is not a name," says Mr. Gradgrind. "Call yourself Cecilia."

She explains that her father calls her Sissy; he insists that her father "has no business to do it." He then proceeds to elicit from her that her father belongs to the "Horseriding," a sort of circus. Again he corrects her, stating that her father must be a horsebreaker, a farrier and veterinary. When she is asked the definition of a horse, she is stumped.

Gradgrind is appalled. She possesses no facts! He calls upon Bitzer to define a horse. Bitzer is a boy with light, cold eyes, light, short-cropped hair, and a skin "so unwholesomely deficient in the natural tinge, that he looked as though, if he were cut, he would bleed white." Bitzer proceeds to define a horse according to the facts: "Quadruped. Graminivorous. Forty teeth, namely twenty-four grinders, four eye-teeth, and twelve incisors." And so forth.

Comment

Dickens is obviously building Sissy and Bitzer into human symbols of the opposing forces. Their descriptions and behavior show this. Sissy is described as dark-haired and dark-eyed, having absorbed "the lustrous color from the sun," while her opposite, Bitzer, is pale, cold, light-eyed, and fair-haired, having had the sun "draw out of him what little color he ever possessed." Sissy, who knows horses intimately, cannot define one; Bitzer, who does not, pleases Gradgrind with his factual definition.

The examination of the pupils is continued by a third man present, a government school-inspector, a personage who "had it in his charge from high authority to bring about the great public-office Millennium, when Commissioners should reign on earth." He wants to know if the children would paper a room with pictures of horses. When half the class respond that they would, he curtly explains that it should not be done because horses do not wander up and down the walls in fact. "Why, then, you are not to see anywhere, what you don't see in fact; you are not to have anywhere, what you don't have in fact. What is called Taste, is only another name for Fact," he lectures them.

To a similar question, that of using a carpet with a design of flowers upon it, "girl number twenty" - Sissy Jupe - still answers that she would like such a carpet. She likes flowers, "the pictures of what was very pretty," and she would fancy. ... "You are never to fancy," is the crushing admonition, seconded by Mr. Gradgrind.

Comment

"Fancy," that is, Imagination, is the enemy of the utilitarian mind. Only that is beautiful or good that is useful. Jerome Buckley in The Victorian Temper describes a critic who condemned a swan-supported table in the Crystal Palace exhibition because no swan in nature would nest under a table.

The proceedings are then turned over to the teacher, Mr. M'Choakumchild, whose teaching technique is to be evaluated by the inspector. The teacher, writes Dickens, is one of some hundred and forty schoolmasters lately turned out "in the same factory, on the same principles, like so many pianoforte legs." At this teachers'-college factory he had been prepared in "orthography, etymology, **syntax**, and **prosody**, biography, astronomy, geography, and general cosmography, the sciences of compound proportion, algebra, land-surveying and leveling, vocal music, and drawing from models. ..." Adds Dickens, "If he had only learnt a little less, how infinitely better he might have taught much more!"

Comment

In his final comment on the dismal schoolmaster, M'Choakumchild (note the apt "tag" name), Dickens shows a concern for education common to many of his novels. To Dickens, the prime requisite for a good education is love for children. Education should also be fun, not all facts. He pictures an ideal school in that of

Dr. Strong in *David Copperfield*, a school in which the boys play games and enjoy learning.

CHAPTER 3: A LOOPHOLE

The school inspection over, Mr. Gradgrind walks homeward "in a state of considerable satisfaction." He wants the children to be model pupils, just as his own children are models. They had been lectured at since they could toddle. They had been indulged in no imaginative fancies. A cow, to them, was not the creature who jumped over the moon (factually impossible), but "a graminivorous ruminating quadruped with several stomachs."

Mr. Gradgrind approaches his house, Stone Lodge, "a great square house, with a heavy portico darkening the principal windows, as its master's heavy eye-brows overshadowed his eyes." All was mathematically exact about the house: an even number of windows, symmetrically distributed; a garden of geometric proportions; all the scientific appliances of the day in place-gas, drainage, water, fire-proofing, mechanical lifts and iron girders.

Inside, he muses, the little Gradgrinds have everything too-scientific, factual collections of seashells, minerals, and metallurgical ores - all labeled and arranged neatly in cabinets. "He was an affectionate father, after his manner," comments Dickens, "... an eminently practical father."

Comment

In Gradgrind's house, as in his appearance, squareness is again the key word. All the practical conveniences the times could provide are there, but the children's rooms are a combination of lecture hall and museum of natural history. He provided everything except the dreams of childhood.

Mr. Gradgrind, approaching his house, passes by Sleary's Horseriding establishment where the sound of music shows that a show is taking place. At the rear of the tent, a group of children are peeping in "at the hidden glories of the place." Gradgrind is annoyed that the circus vagabonds "are attracting the young rabble from a model school." He is horrified to behold that two of them are his own children, Louisa and Thomas. They tell him they wanted to see what the circus was like.

Louisa is a pretty girl of fifteen or sixteen, with a face in which "there was a light with nothing to rest upon, a fire with nothing to burn, a starved imagination keeping life in itself somehow …" She tells her father, "I have been tired a long time." Of what, she can't or won't say. Thomas, in contrast to his sister's sullen defiance, allows himself "to be taken home like a machine." "What would Mr. Bounderby say?" is Gradgrind's final note of disapproval to his two "juvenile delinquents."

Comment

Here is the first hint that the system of education by facts does not work. Even Gradgrind's own carefully lectured children still yearn after "fancy," the world of the imagination represented by the little circus. Louisa's sullen defiance and Thomas' mechanical surrender are suggestions of their future conduct in the novel.

CHAPTER 4: MR. BOUNDERBY

Who is Mr. Bounderby? He is Gradgrind's bosom friend, a man "equally devoid of sentiment." A rich man, a banker and manufacturer, he is a self-made man who vaunts his former poverty and ignorance in a "brassy speaking-trumpet of a voice." He has a "great puffed head," with swollen veins in his temples, and his hair is scant and disorderly, as though "from being constantly blown about by his windy boastfulness."

He stands before the fireplace in the Gradgrind house talking to Mrs. Gradgrind, "a little, thin, white, pink-eyed bundle of shawls, of surpassing feebleness, mental and bodily." Bounderby brags that he had spent his tenth birthday in a ditch and the night in a pigsty. He has reached his present eminence by his determined character and thanks nobody but himself for his rise. He recalls his early history for Mrs. Gradgrind: deserted by his mother, left to his drunken grandmother to be raised, thrown out upon his own resources, he had been a vagabond errand boy in his youth. He is just boasting of his lack of education when Mr. Gradgrind and his young culprits enter.

Comment

Bounderby, the self-made man, is one of the most obnoxious characters in all of Dickens. Just as Gradgrind, the doctrinaire Utilitarian, is characterized by squareness, so Bounderby is described in terms of windiness, flatulence, and brassiness. The deflation of this windbag later on is one of the high points in the novel.

Mrs. Gradgrind sends the children to their rooms "to look at the shells and minerals and things provided" for them, wondering why they would possibly want to see a circus.

Gradgrind is apologetic to Bounderby for the dereliction of his offspring. Something bad has crept into the minds of Louisa and Thomas in spite of their proper training. "The reason is (as you know) the only faculty to which education should be addressed," he tells Bounderby.

Bounderby retorts that an idle imagination is the cause, a bad thing, especially in a girl like Louisa. He suggests that Cecilia (Sissy) Jupe, the circus girl, is the cause of this dangerous stimulation of unwholesome "fancy." She should be expelled from Gradgrind's school.

Gradgrind and Bounderby decide to pay a call on Sissy's father in order to tell him to take his daughter out of school. Before they leave, Bounderby looks in upon the children in their study. He finds Louisa sulkily looking out of the window and Thomas "sniffing revengefully" at the fire. Bounderby plants a kiss on Louisa's cheek in parting. When he has left, she rubs the kissed portion of her face with a handkerchief until it is burning red.

Comment

Two coming events are hinted at here. Sissy is indeed the cause, or at least the representative, of the imagination. Her closeness to Louisa later on will have a profound effect on that girl. Louisa's reaction to Bounderby's kiss is a clue to her later attitude toward him.

CHAPTER 5: THE KEYNOTE

Gradgrind and Bounderby walk through Coketown to seek out Sissy's father. Coketown, "a town of bricks that would have been red if the smoke and ashes had allowed it," is "a triumph of fact," a place without a "taint of fancy in it." A town of machinery, of tall chimneys from which "serpents of smoke trailed themselves forever," of a black canal and "a river that ran purple with ill-smelling dye," its heart is the steam engine which "worked monotonously up and down, like the head of an elephant in a state of melancholy madness." The streets are all alike, "inhabited by people equally like one another," all doing the same work throughout days that are all alike.

Comment

The description of Coketown is that of any one of a number of actual mid-nineteenth-century industrial English cities. The serpents of smoke from the factory chimneys and the mad-elephant engines are animal symbols used by Dickens to signify the brutish evils of industrialized society. Both symbols recur in subsequent chapters.

Coketown also has numerous churches, built by some eighteen different sects, each "a pious warehouse of red brick." The mystery of Coketown, however, is, "who belonged to the eighteen denominations? Because, whoever did, the laboring people did not." The Sunday bells did not call them from their quarters; in fact an organization frequently petitioned Parliament to force these people to become religious. Another organization complained that working people insisted on getting drunk, or taking opium, or frequenting low haunts "where they heard low singing and saw low dancing."

Dickens wonders out loud about the reasons. The people had been deprived, like the little Gradgrinds, of Fancy which demanded "to be brought into healthy existence instead of struggling on in convulsions." The people "worked long and monotonously"; they craved relaxation, something to give them a vent, an outlet, a change.

Comment

Dickens puts his finger prophetically on the sore spot of industrialized life, the deadening monotony of factory work. Because healthy relaxation was unavailable on Sundays, the only day off from work, the working class took to drink and drugs. In his magazine articles Dickens had often attacked the Sabbatarian laws which allowed no public amusements on Sunday. He felt that these were discriminatory because the upper classes could afford private amusements. But the churches, Dickens felt, had lost the working class anyhow. The "pious warehouses" of all denominations offered no living faith to the poor.

As the two men approach Pod's End, where the Jupes live, they are almost run down by Sissy Jupe herself, fleeing from Bitzer, the colorless boy. He has been teasing her about her definition of a horse, she explains. Gradgrind orders Sissy to take them to her father. She is just on her way there, she tells him, carrying a bottle of the "nine oils" with which her father rubs his bruises. They stop at "the door of a mean little public house" where the Jupes live.

CHAPTER 6: SLEARY'S HORSEMANSHIP

Gradgrind and Bounderby follow Sissy up the dimly lit stairs of the inn, the Pegasus' Arms. They are not greeted by the barking of Merrylegs, the Jupes' performing dog, nor by the appearance of Jupe himself. Both are absent from the shabby room. Sissy goes looking for her father on the other floors, but does not find him, and after discovering that his trunk has been emptied, goes out to seek him at another tavern.

The two gentlemen have not gotten over their amazement at her strange behavior, when another surprise overtakes them. A young man, thin-faced, broad-chested but short-legged, appears, smelling of sawdust and horses' provender. He is Mr. E. W. B. Childers, known to circus fans as "The Wild Huntsman of the North American Prairies," and with him is Master Kidderminster, a small boy with an old face, who, properly made up, appears as the huntsman's cupid-like son in their act.

Childers soon informs the two men that they are waiting in vain for the return of Jupe. That performer has of late often "missed his tip" (was fumbling in his acts), has taken to being "goosed" (drunk) because his joints are stiff, and now has "cut" (has run off). In short, Jupe has deserted his daughter. Soon after he had sent her out on an errand (to get her out of the way), he was seen to slink off with a bundle under his arm. He adds that Sissy will never believe that her father has deserted her for he had so doted on her.

Comment

The deserted child is a common character in Dickens' works. From Oliver Twist on, his novels abound with deserted, orphaned, or abused children. In them Dickens is reliving the traumatic experience of his own childhood, when he was "deserted" by his parents by being put to work in a warehouse while his father was in debtor's prison. Dickens is also preparing the groundwork for another point he will make later. Sissy, although abandoned by her father, loves him and is loved by him; Louisa, who has a good home and all the material comforts, does not have love. Her life is ruined by this lack, while Sissy becomes a sort of good fairy, bringing happiness. Love makes all the difference in parent-child relations.

Childers explains that Jupe must have intended to do this all along by putting her in Gradgrind's school and thus seeing her "provided for."

Gradgrind somewhat reluctantly admits that he had come to tell Jupe to take his daughter out of the school, but that his desertion of her has altered things. He will consult with Mr. Bounderby. Soon Mr. Bounderby's brassy voice is heard saying, "No. I say no. I advise you not," while Mr. Gradgrind's is heard replying, "But even as an example to Louisa, of what this pursuit which has been the subject of a vulgar curiosity, leads to and ends, in."

During this debate the various members of Sleary's circus who live in the upstairs room of the inn gather in the hallway. They were "not very tidy in their private dresses," and "not at all orderly in their domestic arrangements." But, writes Dickens, "Yet there was a remarkable gentleness and childishness about these people, a special inaptitude for any kind of sharp practice, and an untiring readiness to help and pity one another, deserving often of as much respect and always of as much generous construction, as the every-day virtues of any class of people in the world."

Comment

The circus people represent the world of the imagination, of "fancy," in contrast to the Gradgrinds, Bounderbys, and others

HARD TIMES

who are the respectable world of facts. Dickens' sympathy is obviously with the former because of their greater humanity. Yet, it must be admitted, the circus people are certainly idealized beyond reality. Dickens' novels, for all their surface **realism**, often have these fairy-tale touches in them.

Mr. Sleary, master of the circus, appears to ask the gentlemen's decision as to Sissy's fate. He is a short man "with one fixed eye, and one loose eye, a voice ... like the efforts of a broken pair of bellows, a flabby surface, and a muddled head which was never sober and never drunk." He addresses Gradgrind as "Thquire" in an asthmatic lisp and states that if Gradgrind can do nothing for Sissy he will take her as a circus apprentice.

Just then Sissy reappears, sees the assembly, but no father, and bursts into tears. "You are gone away for my sake, I am sure!" she cries out. Bounderby, grown impatient from the delay and the emotional scene, brutally interrupts with, "Your father has absconded - deserted you - and you mustn't expect to see him again as long as you live."

At this Sleary mutters to Bounderby that his people are good-natured, but if he doesn't behave better they will pitch him out of the window.

Gradgrind makes peace all around by announcing that although he had come to tell Jupe to take Sissy out of school, "these altered circumstances" have persuaded him to take charge of her, to educate her and provide for her. The only condition is that she is to communicate no more with the circus people.

Sissy accepts, after Gradgrind reminds her that it was her father's wish that she be educated. If her father should return to the circus, no matter where it travels, Mr. Sleary will know of her whereabouts.

The circus women pack up Sissy's meager belongings and bid her a tender farewell. Even the rough men give her a parting kiss, except the child prodigy, Kidderminster, who develops shyness. "Good-bye, my dear!" said Sleary. "You'll make your fortune I hope, and none of our poor folks will ever trouble you. ..." Sissy goes off with the two gentlemen, still clutching the bottle of healing oils she had bought for her father, for "he will want it when he comes back."

Comment

In deciding to become Sissy's guardian, over the opposition of Bounderby, Gradgrind has shown his first spark of humanity. He of course does not admit this, but thinks he is only doing this to save the girl from a life of "fancy" and idleness. In the end, this decision proves to be his salvation in reconciling him with his own daughter.

CHAPTER 7: MRS. SPARSIT

Over the bachelor establishment of Bounderby rules Mrs. Sparsit, an elderly lady with a Coriolanian nose and dense black eyebrows. She is the widow of a man who had died of too much brandy long ago, but who enjoys powerful family connections among the Powlers and Scadgers, local aristocracy. Mrs. Sparsit never tires of reminding people of her better days and her lofty social station. Mr. Bounderby, the self-made man who boasts of his own low background, boasts just as proudly of his housekeeper's exalted station. She is his foil, his "captive princess," to demonstrate his own achieved superiority.

Mr. Bounderby is having breakfast and is thinking about Gradgrind's whim "of bringing up the tumbling girl." She has been staying at his house until Gradgrind can decide whether to let her live with his family as a companion to Louisa. Bounderby harbors fatherly feelings toward the Gradgrind children; in fact, he tells Mrs. Sparsit he is going to take young Tom into his office after the boy has finished his schooling. He takes the opportunity to expound in his usual fashion how there had been no one to take him under his wing, or give him an education. Mrs. Sparsit, he avers, was at the Italian opera while he hadn't a penny and slept on the pavements. She was born in the lap of luxury, was in "devilish high society," and he is glad she likes to hear "what Josiah Bounderby, of Coketown, has gone through." She agrees to everything.

Comment

Bounderby, with this constant reference to his low origins and the hardness of his early life, poses as a humble man, but is really one type of snob. His feelings of self-aggrandizement must be constantly fed by contrasting his present power and wealth with his former poverty. He likes Mrs. Sparsit about him and constantly elicits from her statements of her former high station and luxurious life, because she is now his servant and he can enjoy his superiority over her.

Mr. Gradgrind and his daughter come to take Sissy home with them. Sissy is sent for, and on entering the room she curtseys to all except Mrs. Sparsit, whom she overlooks in her confusion. Bounderby immediately reprimands her with the remark that he comes of the scum of the earth, but that Mrs. Sparsit is "a highly connected lady" and demands respect.

Gradgrind suggests that Sissy's dereliction is only an oversight. He then turns to the girl to announce that he has made up his mind to take her into his house. When not at school she is to attend upon Mrs. Gradgrind, "who is rather an invalid." "I have explained to Miss Louisa," he continues, "... the miserable but natural end of your late career; and you are to expressly understand that the whole of this subject is past, and is not to be referred to anymore. From this time you begin your history." He continues, "You will be reclaimed and reformed." Thus it was when Mr. Gradgrind and Louisa took Cecilia Jupe off to Stone Lodge with them.

Comment

Gradgrind tells Sissy that she is to be reclaimed and reformed. Actually it is he who will eventually be reclaimed and reformed by the girl's greater humanity.

CHAPTER 8: NEVER WONDER

"Let us strike the key-note again, before pursuing the tune," writes Dickens. Some six years before the **episode** in the last chapter, Louisa had been overheard by her father to say to her brother, "Tom, I wonder. ..." Mr. Gradgrind had promptly interrupted with, "Louisa, never wonder!"

This, writes Dickens, is the "spring of the mechanical art and mystery of educating the reason without stooping to the cultivation of the sentiments and affections." Settle everything by arithmetic and never wonder. Mr. M'Choakumchild, the Gradgrind schoolmaster, echoes this philosophy. "Bring to me ... yonder baby just able to walk, and I will engage that it shall never wonder." The eighteen denominations which made up the religious structure of Coketown quarreled over everything, but all agreed that children are never to wonder.

Yet people kept on wondering. "They wondered about human nature, human passions, human hopes and fears, the struggles, triumphs and defeats, the cares and joys and sorrows, the lives and deaths of common men and women!" After the fifteen hours of a day's work they went to the Coketown library "to read mere fables about men and women, more or less like themselves. ... " They preferred novels to geometry or political economy.

Comment

Dickens again belabors the point that the working classes need and want imaginative relaxation after their monotonous day's work, not educational facts and figures. Gradgrindism denies them this solace.

One night after Sissy has come to live with the Gradgrinds, Tom says to his sister Louisa, "I am sick of my life, Loo. I hate it altogether, and I hate everybody except you." He hates having to call Sissy "Jupe" and notices that she is getting as pale as wax in "this-jolly old-Jaundiced Jail."

Louisa responds that she wishes she could better reconcile Tom to their home. "I can't talk to you so as to lighten your mind, for I never see any amusing sights or read any amusing books that it would be a pleasure or a relief to you to talk about, when you are tired."

Tom replies that he wishes he could put all the Facts and Figures "and all the people who found them out" someplace, put gunpowder under them and blow them all up. "However, when I go to live with old Bounderby, I'll have my revenge," he concludes.

When asked how he expects to revenge himself, he says, "I mean, I'll enjoy myself a little, and go about and see something, and hear something. I'll recompense myself for this way in which I have been brought up."

Comment

Tom's disgust at his mode of life and Louisa's sorrow that she cannot help Tom enjoy life better are **foreshadowing** of things to come. Louisa later marries Bounderby only to please Tom and smooth his way. Tom revenges himself by absconding with Bounderby's money.

Tom continues to prophesy his future with Bounderby. He knows how to manage him, he asserts; he will use the man's obvious liking for Louisa as a tool.

Louisa stares silently into the fire. She asks Tom at last why he looks forward so much to working with Bounderby. He replies that at least there he can put her influence to advantage, a thing not of much use at home.

Mrs. Gradgrind enters the room and puts an end to the brooding. After all the lectures and experiments they have had, to just sit there and "wonder." Their father would be disturbed by this and she would never hear the end of it. "I wish," she whimpers, "yes, I do wish that I had never had a family, and then you would have known what it was to do without me."

Comment

Mrs. Gradgrind's final statement is one of the meager attempts at humor in this, Dickens' least funny book.

HARD TIMES

TEXTUAL ANALYSIS

BOOK 1: SOWING, CHAPTERS 9-16

CHAPTER 9: SISSY'S PROGRESS

Sissy Jupe is having a difficult time between Mrs. Gradgrind and Mr. M'Choakumchild; she often has the desire to run away. Only the thought that her father had not really abandoned her, that he would return, and had wished her to remain at school, keeps her from leaving. The teacher reported that "she had a very dense head for figures," and that when asked for the first principle of political economy she had replied, "To do unto others as I would that they should do unto me." This will not do.

One night Sissy asks Louisa to help her with her schoolwork. She cannot understand a recent lesson on National Prosperity. The teacher had asked for a "statistical proportion relative to twenty-five people who starved to death out of a population of one million." Sissy had replied that "it must be just as hard upon those who were starved, whether the others were a million, or a million million." That, of course, was not the correct answer; that was not a fact.

Comment

Dickens continues to ridicule the cold, inhuman statistical approach to social problems by making it the curriculum of Gradgrind's school. The pain of death by hunger is not made less for the victims by consoling them with a low percentage factor for death by starvation. He also suggests that the Golden Rule might perhaps be a good first principle of political economy.

The conversation then is turned by Louisa to forbidden ground, Sissy's past, of which she was never to speak. Louisa asks Sissy about her father and mother. She replies that her mother, a dancer, had died when she was born. Her father, a clown, traveled the country with the circus. Lately he had not always succeeded in making people laugh. He would come home in despair, and once he had even beaten poor little Merrylegs, his performing dog. On the day he left, he had been especially depressed. She had found him crying.

At this point Tom appears to tell Louisa that Bounderby is here and that she should come down so that, pleased, he would invite Tom to dinner. Dickens observes that Tom "was becoming that not unprecedented triumph of calculation which is usually at work on number one ...," a selfish, spoiled youth.

Sissy causes annoyance to the Gradgrinds by frequently asking if a letter has come with news of her father. Mr. Gradgrind regularly replies that no word has come. After she leaves the room with trembling lips, he adds that if she had been properly brought up she would realize the "baselessness of these fantastic hopes." Mrs. Gradgrind whines that her poor head is "vexed and worried" by Jupe's tiresome letters.

Comment

Tom is being built up by Dickens more and more into the heartless, self-seeking egoist. When Tom plays upon Louisa's love for him to have her marry the odious Bounderby, we are not too surprised. Tom is, after all, utilitarianism in action, the end product of an inhumane education.

CHAPTER 10: STEPHEN BLACKPOOL

In the darkest heart of Coketown, in "a labyrinth of narrow courts," where "the killing airs and gases were bricked in," lives a certain Stephen Blackpool. Although he is forty years of age, he looks older with his stooping gait, knotted brow, and "hard-looking head … on which the iron-grey hair lay long and thin." He is not particularly intelligent, nor gifted with speech, but merely "a good power-loom weaver, and a man of perfect integrity."

One night when the factories have closed and the "hands" are all hurrying home, Stephen is standing in the street waiting for a certain young woman. At last out of the parade of shawled figures one comes forward. It is Rachael, a woman with a "quiet oval face, dark and rather delicate, irradiated by a pair of very gentle eyes, and further set off by the perfect order of her shining black hair." She is not a girl, but a woman of about thirty-five.

HARD TIMES

She admonishes Stephen that they shouldn't be seen so often walking together, even though they are "such old friends, and getting to be such old folk, now."

He replies that she has been his friend so many years, has heartened and cheered him, and that her word is law to him, more so than the laws of the land which are a "muddle." Life's problems are a muddle, he says, "I come to the muddle many times and agen, and I never get beyond it."

Comment

"'Tis a muddle," is Stephen Blackpool's tag line. Like Mr. Micawber's "Something will turn up," in *David Copperfield*, it sums up his philosophy. Stephen Blackpool represents the decent workingman who is in a mental muddle when he thinks about the mass of contradictions that Victorian society has become. As a character, Stephen is not too well drawn. His Lancashire dialect is almost unintelligible to most readers and his behavior is rather implausible, or at least poorly motivated. Rachael, his female counterpart strangely enough does not speak the same dialect, although as a worker in a Lancashire town she presumably is also a native.

Stephen drops Rachael off at her place and then goes to his home. He lives over a little shop in whose window "wretched little toys" are mixed with "cheap newspapers and pork. ..." He enters his room, a clean place with decent furniture and a few books. As he places his candle upon a table he stumbles over "a disabled, drunken creature, barely able to preserve her sitting posture." She is grimy, in tatters, and she tries to push her tangled hair from her face as she greets Stephen. "Back agen ever and ever so often. Back? Yes, back. Why not?" she screeches at him.

She staggers toward the bed, falls drunkenly upon it, and is soon asleep, snoring. Stephen sinks into a chair and moves from it only once during the night to throw a cover over his guest.

Comment

The identity of the mysterious visitor will soon be revealed and it will explain the sadness of the relationship between Stephen and Rachael. The device of introducing a character whose identity is not immediately revealed is often used by Dickens to arouse suspense. It was common in the nineteenth-century novel.

CHAPTER 11: NO WAY OUT

In the morning "the monstrous serpents of smoke" again trail over Coketown, and the "melancholy mad elephants" of steam engines work again, "oiled up for the day's monotony." Stephen works steadily at his loom. "In the waste-yard outside, the steam from the escape pipes, the litter of barrels and old iron, the shiny heaps of cools, the ashes everywhere, were shrouded in a veil of mist and rain."

When the noon bell rings for the lunch hour, Stephen turns his steps toward the hill where his employer lives in a red brick house with his name Bounderby "upon a brazen plate, and a round brazen door-handle underneath it, like a brazen full-stop."

HARD TIMES

> **Comment**

Notice how references to Bounderby are all in metallic symbols. Not only are the door accessories of Bounderby's house brazen, he himself is.

Stephen is admitted to see Bounderby, who is lunching upon a chop with sherry wine, with Mrs. Sparsit ministering to him. Bounderby feels magnanimous toward his "hand" Blackpool, for he is not one of those who "expect to be set up in a coach and six, and to be fed on turtle-soup and venison, with a gold spoon." This, Bounderby is sure, is the secret longing of most workers.

Stephen explains that he has come to ask advice of his employer in regard to his marriage. He has been married nineteen years, but his wife went bad. Many times she had pawned the furniture and clothing for drinks. Finally she had left him, although he had been so patient with her. For the past five years he had paid her to keep away from him. Last night he had found her again in his room. What is he to do?

Bounderby coldly replies that he has heard all this sort of thing before and that Stephen should never have married.

Mrs. Sparsit breaks into the conversation to inquire rather pointedly whether there had been a great difference in the ages of Stephen and his wife. She seems disappointed when he tells her that it is not so.

> **Comment**

Mrs. Sparsit, who suspects Bounderby's interest in Louisa to be matrimonial, is here attempting to use Stephen's misfortune as a means of discouraging Bounderby. Bounderby is more than twice Louisa's age.

Stephen at last blurts out that what he wants to know is how to be rid of his drunken derelict of a wife so he can marry Rachael. Mrs. Sparsit is "much dejected by the immorality of the people," now revealed, while Bounderby can only remind Stephen that he took her "for better or worse."

Stephen states that he has read that great folk "are not bonded together for better or worse so fast, but that they can be set free fro' their misfortnet marriages, an' marry ower agen." Even if they cannot get along while married, they at least have so much room in their houses that they can live apart. The poor, like himself, have only one room to live in.

Bounderby states that there is no way for Stephen to be rid of his wife. He will be punished by the law if he deserts her, punished by the law if he hurts her, punished if he marries another, and punished if he lives with the other woman without marrying her.

"Now, a' God's name," pleads Stephen Blackpool, "show me the law to help me!" "There is such a law," counters Bounderby, "but it is not for you at all. It costs money … a mint of money. … I suppose from 1000 to 1500 pounds." Stephen turns white and dejectedly says, "'Tis just a muddle a'toogether, an' the sooner I am dead, the better."

Comment

This attack on the unyielding rigidity of British divorce laws has both social and personal significance for Dickens. His reformer's conscience was disturbed at the injustice by which only the wealthy could obtain a divorce by a special Act of Parliament. At the same time his own relations with his wife were already strained. He was to separate from her in 1858, but he never obtained a divorce.

CHAPTER 12: THE OLD WOMAN

As Stephen descends the steps of Bounderby's house he meets "an old woman, tall and shapely still, though withered by time." She is cleanly and plainly dressed, carries an umbrella and a basket, and seems to be from the country on a rare visit to town.

She asks Stephen about Bounderby and he has the feeling from the way she carries herself that he has seen her before, "and had not quite liked her." She tells him that she comes to Coketown once a year just to look at Bounderby from afar and to see how he is. She becomes rather chatty, and talks to Stephen about his job in Bounderby's factory. Later, when he has returned to his loom, he looks out of the window and sees the old woman standing outside, looking at the mill, "lost in admiration."

Comment

The identity of this mysterious, unnamed woman, the second to appear, will not be divulged until Chapter 5 of Book 3. A careful reader might make a shrewd guess even now as to her identity. Dickens is not overly subtle.

When he leaves work that night, there is no Rachael on the corner to walk home with. Depressed by her absence, he trudges wearily homeward, thinking how different his life might have been had he married Rachael. "He thought of the waste of the best part of his life, of the change it made in his character for the worse every day, of the dreadful nature of his existence, bound hand and foot to a dead woman, and tormented by a demon in her shape. He thought of Rachael, how young when they were first brought together in these circumstances, how mature now, how soon to grow old."

Comment

This short chapter is a good example of the technique used by Dickens to end a weekly installment. Notice how suspense is built up in two ways: the appearance of the mysterious old woman who is so curious about Bounderby, the unexplained absence of Rachael from her customary meeting place. The reader looks forward to next week's installment in order to find out more.

CHAPTER 13: RACHAEL

Stephen gloomily enters his home, and is surprised to find Rachael sitting by the bed. She is tending Stephen's wife, for the landlady had called her to take care of the ill woman who had once worked beside her when both had been young girls. Rachael dresses her sores with a lotion left by the physician, a liquid whose label shows it to be a deadly poison if taken internally. Rachael tells Stephen that his wife will come to her senses by tomorrow. Meanwhile she will sit up with her, and Stephen should sleep in the chair.

As he dozes off he sees Rachael "as if she had a glory shining round her head." He has a fitful dream of standing in a church being married, but not to Rachael, and the congregation is a vast crowd of people with unpitying eyes. The scene shifts and he is now standing beneath his own loom and the ceremonies have changed to a burial service for him.

He awakens to find that Rachael has dozed off and that his wife from behind the bed curtains is groping for the medicine bottle. Motionless, powerless to move, he sees his wife pour a mug full of the poisonous lotion. Just as she is about to drink the fatal draught, Rachael awakes and seizes it from her.

Early the next morning, Rachael leaves. "Thou art an angel. Bless thee, bless thee!" Stephen murmurs to her. "Thou'rt an Angel; it may be, thou hast saved my soul alive!" Who knows, he continues, what he might have done to his wife or himself with the poison bottle, had Rachael not been here.

Comment

The emotion-filled wake at the bedside of Stephen's alcoholic derelict of a wife seems overdone for the tastes of modern readers. Yet this kind of bathos is exactly what endeared Dickens to his audience. They expected scenes like this from him.

Stephen's dream is prophetic. He will find, not marriage to Rachael, but death, in a subsequent chapter. Dickens is here setting us up for this **climax** to come.

CHAPTER 14: THE GREAT MANUFACTURER

"Time went on in Coketown," writes Dickens, "like its own machinery..." But time did go on, and one day Mr. Gradgrind was forced to observe, "Louisa is becoming almost a young woman." Time also had made young Thomas Gradgrind a young man with a long-tailed coat, stiff collar, and his first razor. He duly joined Bounderby's banking house, as planned. Time, "the great manufacturer," also worked on Sissy Jupe, making her "up into a very pretty article indeed."

Mr. Gradgrind decides that the continuance of Sissy at his school is useless. She is deplorably deficient in facts, has only a very limited acquaintance with figures, and is "altogether backward and below the mark." Sissy, confronted, admits all this, but claims that she has always tried hard. Gradgrind concurs, but adds in her defense, "You are an affectionate, earnest, good young woman - and - and we must make that do." Gradgrind "really liked Sissy too well to have a contempt for her"; she possessed some indefinable quality beyond his ability to tabulate, calculate, or divide.

Comment

Dickens is gradually allowing Gradgrind to mellow from his hard-bitten Utilitarianism. Although Gradgrind does not realize it, the influence for change is the presence of Sissy Jupe in his household.

Time has worked on Mr. Gradgrind too, and made him a Member of Parliament for Coketown, serving on a commission for facts.

One night soon after his discovery that Louisa has become a woman, he tells her that he wishes to have a serious talk with her the next morning. Louisa sits musing, looking at the dying embers of the fire in the grate, when her brother Tom enters.

HARD TIMES

He wants to know if their father had spoken to her. He tells her that Bounderby and their father are together this night, "having a regular confab."

Suddenly Tom asks Louisa if she is very fond of him. It would be jolly, a splendid thing for him, if she were to make up her mind when asked, with her love for him in view. He hints rather mysteriously that "something is going on," but as he is to go out with some fellows, he cannot stay to tell her more. "You won't forget how fond you are of me?" he asks in departing. "No, dear Tom, I won't forget," she replies.

Comment

The reader can guess that Gradgrind is going to marry Louisa off to Bounderby, and that she will agree to the odious match out of love for her self-seeking brother. Tom is by now revealed as a thoroughgoing egoist, using his sister's love for him only to further the career of "number one" - himself.

CHAPTER 15: FATHER AND DAUGHTER

In the morning Louisa dutifully appears in her father's study, "a stern room, with a deadly statistical clock in it, which measured every second with a beat like a rap upon a coffin-lid." In this room, "with its abundance of blue books," the most complicated social questions "were cast up, got into exact totals, and finally settled."

Mr. Gradgrind asks Louisa to pay the most serious attention to what he is about to say to her. "You are not impulsive, you are not romantic, you are accustomed to view everything from the strong dispassionate ground of reason and calculation. From that ground alone, I know you will view and consider what I am going to communicate."

She says nothing and keeps silent even after he tells her that she is the subject of a proposal for marriage. He is rather discomposed by her silence, and goes on to tell her that it is Mr. Bounderby who wishes to make her his wife.

At last Louisa asks, "Do you think I love Mr. Bounderby?" When her father replies that he cannot say so, she asks again, "Do you ask me to love Mr. Bounderby?" He can only splutter that the word "love" may be misplaced, a fancy. Let us look at the facts instead, he states. She is twenty; Bounderby is fifty. They are perhaps apart in years, but equal in means and position. Statistics show, he goes on, that husbands are usually older than wives. That is sufficient.

Still unemotional, Louisa asks her father, "Shall I marry him?" When he replies that the decision is hers to make upon the stated facts, just as his own marriage to her mother was made by practical minds, there comes an instant "when she was impelled to throw herself upon his breast, and give him the pent-up confidences of her heart." But, writes Dickens, Gradgrind was blind to this moment because of "the artificial barriers he had for many years been erecting, between himself and all those subtle essences of humanity. ..."

Comment

The tragedy of Louisa's unfortunate marriage might still have been averted at this point had Gradgrind shown a modicum of human sympathy, or Louisa a bit of resistance. As it is, both have been conditioned to do what they did by the philosophy of "facts."

Dickens is also attacking the typical middle- or upper-class arranged marriage in which financial considerations, not love, play the deciding role.

She tells her father that she accepts. "Since Mr. Bounderby likes to take me thus, I am satisfied to accept his proposal." It is immaterial to her, she adds, when the wedding is to take place.

Her father wants to know whether she has ever had other proposals in secret. She reassures him that her heart has had no experience, that she knows nothing of "tastes and fancies; of aspirations and affections. ..." You have been so careful of me, that I never had a child's heart. You have trained me so well, that I never dreamed a child's dream," she tells him. Gradgrind obtusely accepts this as testimony to his success as parent and educator (when in reality it is a damning indictment of his failure, as later events will demonstrate).

They go down together to tell the news to Mrs. Gradgrind. That languid vegetable-like person has only one worry over her daughter's impending marriage: what is she to call Mr. Bounderby? She does not like his first name, Josiah; she cannot call such an imposing personage Joe; she will not call him Mister. She hopes that the wedding will be soon, for otherwise she won't hear the end of it.

Only Sissy, who is present at this scene, gives Louisa a look of sympathy and sorrow. Louisa, catching it, turns cold, proud, and impassive toward her from that moment on.

Comment

The lack of love in the Gradgrind household is further revealed in the reaction of Mrs. Gradgrind to the news of Louisa's marriage. Her only concern seems to be that it might upset the routine of her life. She and Louisa have apparently never been close, exchanged confidences, or had a normal parent-child relationship. Louisa can communicate with her no more than with her father.

Sissy, who has human sympathy, senses that Louisa's marriage is not to be based on love and pities her for it. Louisa, ashamed and discomfited at being found out, turns against her at this point.

CHAPTER 16: HUSBAND AND WIFE

Mr. Bounderby is troubled by the necessity of telling his housekeeper, Mrs. Sparsit, about his impending marriage. He is not sure how to tell her, or how she would take it. She might even depart for Lady Scadgers, her wealthy relation, or "be plaintive or abusive, tearful or tearing."

Once he has decided that the ordeal could no longer be avoided, he takes the precaution of buying a large bottle of smelling salts on the way home. He enters his house and "appeared before the object of his misgivings, like a dog who was conscious of coming direct from the pantry."

Comment

The blustering Bounderby's uneasy conscience toward Mrs. Sparsit is somewhat puzzling. Had he perhaps allowed her to entertain thoughts that he might marry her? Has she been more than a housekeeper to him? With Victorian reticence Dickens never develops these points further.

After he has paid Mrs. Sparsit his usual compliments and adds that she is "not only a lady born and bred, but a devilish sensible woman," he breaks the news to her.

To his utter amazement she replies only that she hopes he may be happy. "And she said it with such great condescension as well as with such great compassion, that Bounderby ..." was more disconcerted than had she "swooned on the hearthrug." "Somehow," adds Dickens, "she seemed in a moment, to have established a right to pity him ever afterward."

Comment

Just as the low-born Bounderby delights in having a "high-born lady" for a housekeeper, a form of snobbery on his part, so Mrs. Sparsit really despises her employer as a vulgar upstart. We shall see, however, that her pity is not misplaced.

It is arranged that Mrs. Sparsit will move to an apartment over Bounderby's bank, will have a maid to attend upon her and a porter to protect her (and the bank), an arrangement she accepts with great condescension. No matter how Bounderby blusters, she "resolved to have compassion on him as a Victim. ..." "She had that tenderness for his melancholy fate, that his great red countenance used to break out into cold perspiration when she looked at him."

The wedding has been planned for eight weeks from hence, and "Mr. Bounderby went every evening to Stone Lodge as an accepted wooer. Love was made on these occasions in the form of bracelets; and, on all occasions during the period of betrothal, took on a manufacturing aspect." Dresses, cakes, financial settlements were all made. "The business was all Facts, from first to last."

At last the wedding day arrives and the ceremony goes off without any nonsense. At the breakfast which follows, Josiah Bounderby delivers himself of an address to the assembled guests. He reminds them that little did he think when he was a ragged street urchin that he would once marry the daughter of Tom Gradgrind, Member of Parliament. He has long watched the girl growing up and believes that she is worthy of him.

Before Louisa leaves on her honeymoon to Lyons (where her husband wishes to inspect labor relations), she meets her brother Tom briefly in the hall. He whispers that she is a game girl, "a first-rate sister." She clings to him briefly, and "was a little shaken in her reserved composure for the first time."

Comment

Louisa has entered this loveless marriage only to please her selfish brother. Bounderby has married to feed his colossal self-esteem with another female trophy, symbolic of his social rise. Mr. Gradgrind has made an alliance with the richest and most powerful man in Coketown. Tom has a guarantee of a good career as Bounderby's brother-in-law. Everything is eminently practical, yet it is also doomed to failure. The meaning of the title of Book 1, "Sowing," now is apparent.

HARD TIMES

TEXTUAL ANALYSIS

BOOK 2: REAPING, CHAPTERS 1-6

CHAPTER 1: EFFECTS IN THE BANK

It is a hot midsummer day and "Coketown lay shrouded in a haze of its own, which appeared impervious to the sun's rays." As always, the mill owners complained that they were by being ruined by being "required to send laboring children to school; they were ruined, when inspectors were appointed to look into their works; they were ruined, when such inspectors considered it doubtful whether they were quite justified in chopping people up with their machinery; they were utterly undone, when it was hinted that perhaps they need not always make so much smoke." The mill owners on these occasions would threaten that rather than suffer this interference with their property, they would pitch it into the Atlantic. However, they never did, "but, on the contrary" were "kind enough to take good care of it" so that "it increased and multiplied."

Comment

Dickens is referring to the various pieces of legislation such as the Factory Acts which cut working hours, provided released time for education, and forced the factory owners to put safeguards on dangerous machinery. These Acts, along with the early attempts to control smoke pollution, were much opposed by the laissez faire capitalists as undue infringements on their private property rights.

On one such hot day when "the whole town seemed to be frying in oil," only the "melancholy mad elephants," the steam engines, went on unperturbed by the temperature. Mrs. Sparsit sits in her apartment over the bank, "on the shadier side of the frying street." Her coming to the bank has "shed a feminine, not to say also aristocratic, grace upon the office." She presides over its various vaults, iron rooms, and even a "little armory of cutlasses and carbines," aided by a deaf serving woman and the light porter, who is none other than Bitzer, the fellow who had once properly defined a horse for girl number twenty.

One evening when all has been shut up, Mrs. Sparsit condescends to chat with Bitzer on the news of the day. She hears that the workers are uniting with one another, to which she comments, "It is much to be regretted ... that the united masters allow of any such class-combinations. "She continues, "I only know that these people must be conquered, and that it's high time it was done."

Comment

As a member of the upper class, Mrs. Sparsit has no understanding of the "lower orders," as they were then called. She can see no justice in their forming a union to protect themselves against their united exploiters. Dickens' **irony** in allowing her to put forth her class view earned him Macaulay's reproach that *Hard Times* smacked of "sullen Socialism."

Bitzer continues his news commentary by mentioning that all the clerks are "trustworthy, punctual, and industrious," except one-young Thomas Gradgrind. Mrs. Sparsit reproaches him for mentioning the name, connected as it now is to that of their employer. But she is eager anyway to hear more. Tom, relates Bitzer, "is a dissipated, extravagant idler … not worth his salt." He would not get on at all at the Bank had he not "a friend and relation at court." Bitzer hopes that this friend and relation is not the one supplying him "with the means of carrying on," for then we would know "out of whose pocket that money comes."

Bitzer, Dickens comments, is the general spy and informer in Bounderby's establishment and is duly rewarded at Christmas for it with a bonus. "He had grown into an extremely clearheaded, cautious, prudent young man, who was safe to rise in the world. His mind was so exactly regulated, that he had no affections or passions." On his father's death, he had promptly put his mother into the workhouse, in which place he generously allowed her the luxury of a half pound of tea per year as his contribution to her welfare.

Comment

Both young Tom and Bitzer are the products of Gradgrind's utilitarian education. Both are utterly selfish (devoted only to number one, themselves), calculating, and ruthless in relation to others.

Bitzer continues expounding his philosophy of life to Mrs. Sparsit. He saves much of his wages, needing no recreation or family, and he cannot see why the factory "hands" want them. By "watching and informing upon one another" they too "could earn a trifle now and then, whether in money or goodwill, and improve their livelihood."

There is a knock on the door, and a gentleman is shown in after Mrs. Sparsit has had the opportunity of composing her "classical features." She meets him "in the manner of a Roman matron going outside the city walls to treat with an invading general."

Her visitor is as haughty as she, although in a different manner. He is unmoved by her "impressive entry," and stands "whistling to himself will all imaginable coolness. ..." There is "a certain air of exhaustion upon him" as though "from excessive gentility." He is "a thorough gentleman, made to the model of the time, weary of everything, and putting no more faith in anything than Lucifer."

Comment

Dickens is loading the dice against Mr. James Harthouse (for that turns out to be his name) from the start. Harthouse, the effete aristocrat, represents another type of snob to add to the collection made up of Bounderby and Mrs. Sparsit.

Mrs. Sparsit observes the visitor to be a man of about thirty-five, handsome, dark-haired, well-bred, and well-dressed. The gentleman bears a letter from Mr. Gradgrind in London introducing him to Mr. Bounderby of Coketown.

He has heard, he says, that Mr. Bounderby is married to Gradgrind's daughter. Is it true that the lady is "quite a philosopher ... absolutely unapproachable ... repellently and stunningly clever?" Is she forty or forty-five? When he sees by Mrs. Sparsit's smile that the answer to all these troubled queries is No, he seems relieved. Her father's description had prepared him to find "a grim and stony maturity" in Mrs. Bounderby.

After the gentleman leaves, Mrs. Sparsit sits long at her window gazing at the murky sun setting over Coketown. "O, you Fool," she says at last.

Comment

The stranger's (Mr. Harthouse) curiosity about the wife of Bounderby is a hint of his future involvement with her. Mrs. Sparsit's final epithet, "You Fool," is addressed to Bounderby, whose marriage to Louisa she does not approve of. Her womanly intuition may also suggest to her that the handsome young stranger will make a fool of Bounderby with his young wife.

CHAPTER 2: MR. JAMES HARTHOUSE

Dickens gives us a little background to explain the appearance in Coketown of the languid gentleman, Mr. James Harthouse. "The Gradgrind party [the Utilitarians or Manchester economists] wanted assistance ... went about recruiting; and where could they enlist recruits more hopefully, than among the fine gentlemen ...?" The Gradgrinds "liked fine gentlemen; they pretended that they did not, but they did." They imitated their speech and manners, and in time there developed "a wonderful hybrid race."

BRIGHT NOTES STUDY GUIDE

One of their recruits among the gentlemen of "good family" is the younger brother of a Member of Parliament, a young man who had been bored as a Cornet of Dragoons, bored as assistant to an ambassador, bored by yachting and travels. He coached himself upon a few texts in statistics and was pronounced ready to take a useful place in the Coketown establishment. Thus was it that James Harthouse, Esquire, appeared one day before Josiah Bounderby, the great Coketown magnate.

Comment

Dickens does not pursue much further this **theme** of the unholy alliance between the rising capitalist middle class and the ruling upper class. It is obvious, however, even from this slight introduction, that Dickens despises both groups and holds them jointly responsible for the woes of the working class.

Mr. Bounderby lectures Mr. Harthouse on the situation in Coketown: its smoke "is the healthiest thing in the world," the work in the mills is "the pleasantest work there is" as well as "the lightest" and "the best paid." Yet, all the "Hands" have as their ultimate objective in life only "to be fed on turtle-soup and venison with a gold spoon."

Mr. Harthouse professes to agree with "this condensed epitome of the whole Coketown question." The two men then go to Mr. Bounderby's house, where Mr. Harthouse is to meet Mrs. Bounderby. He finds her to be "the most remarkable girl ... he had ever seen." She is "reserved and yet so watchful; so cold and proud, and yet so sensitively ashamed of her husband's braggart humility. ..." Her home gives no appearance of a woman in the house; "no graceful little adornment, no fanciful little device, however trivial, anywhere expressed her influence."

The rooms are "cheerless and comfortless, boastfully and doggedly rich. ..."

Comment

That the childhood lessons learned in Gradgrind's school against flowers in the carpet and horses on the wallpaper would result in this kind of interior decorating is now made obvious. Besides, Louisa, we are given to understand, has never made it her home really; it is Bounderby's house just as she is Bounderby's wife, both his possessions and status symbols.

Bounderby introduces Harthouse to Louisa by telling him that she has "lots of expensive knowledge" and that if he should want to cram for any subject, Louisa would be a good adviser. They should get together often.

Louisa talks to Harthouse about his future political career with Gradgrind's party. It turns out that he has no beliefs, no opinions, in fact has a conviction "that any set of ideas will do just as much good as any other set, and just as much harm as any other set." He is attached to the side which will assure him the best chance for success. "You are a singular politician," says Louisa.

Comment

Gradgrind, for all of his obtuse perversity, has at least the strength of his convictions in his beliefs. He is doctrinaire perhaps, but sincere in his socio-political faith. Harthouse is a mere opportunist, empty of all ideology except personal aggrandizement.

In the evening the dinner table is set for four; the fourth turns out to be young Thomas Gradgrind. Harthouse notes how Louisa's eyes light up when she sees her brother. "This whelp is the only creature she cares for," he observes to himself. Harthouse proceeds to encourage Tom's acquaintance and even gets him to escort him back to his hotel after dinner.

CHAPTER 3: THE WHELP

"It was very remarkable," comments Dickens, "that a young gentleman who had been brought up under one continuous system of unnatural restraint, should be a hypocrite; but it was certainly the case with Tom." He was also incapable of governing himself, and in spite of his strangled imagination, a prey to "groveling sensualism."

Tom is quickly persuaded by his new friend, the sumptuous Mr. Harthouse, to come up for a drink and a smoke. Tom is impressed by the man's air of negligent ease. "What an easy swell he is!" he mused in admiration. The conversation soon turns to Tom's brother-in-law, Mr. Bounderby. Tom admits candidly that he does not like him, and adds that his sister never cared for him either. When Harthouse, flicking the ash from his cigar, states coolly, "We are in the present tense now," Tom replies that his sister does not care for Bounderby presently.

Harthouse professes astonishment, for, "What am I bound to suppose, when I find two married people living in harmony and happiness?" Tom, who by this time has assumed an air of easy familiarity with Harthouse, confides to him that Louisa married Bounderby at her father's suggestion. But Louisa, he adds, would not have been so dutiful had it not been for him. "I persuaded her," he says. "I was stuck into old Bounderby's bank (where I never wanted to be), ... so I told her my wishes, and she came into them. She would do anything for me." She gets on alright now, has settled down to the life, for after all "she's not a common sort of girl."

Harthouse tells Tom that he has met Mrs. Sparsit when inquiring at the Bank for Bounderby's address. Tom then volunteers the information that Mrs. Sparsit has affection and devotion for Louisa, for she has never set her cap for her employer. After this bit of dubious observation, Tom falls asleep from too much drink and cigars. When he finally rouses himself to go home, he is not free of the "impression of the presence and influence of his new friend."

Comments Dickens, "If he had had any sense of what he had done that night, and had been less of a whelp and more of a brother, he might have turned short on the road, might have gone down to the ill-smelling river ... and have curtained his head forever with its filthy waters."

Comment

In Harthouse, Dickens introduces another villain, a ne'er-do-well aristocrat, political careerist, and effete sensualist. The highly personal information about his sister which Tom gives Harthouse will be used to bring her almost to the brink of adultery. This is her selfish brother's supreme betrayal, the ultimate result of his loveless, practical upbringing.

CHAPTER 4: MEN AND BROTHERS

"Oh my friends, the down-trodden operatives of Coketown! Oh my friends and fellow-countrymen, the slaves of an iron-handed and a grinding despotism!" So begins the harangue of an "ill-made, high-shouldered man, with lowering brows, and his features crushed into an habitually sour expression." He tells the crowd of workers assembled in the gas-lit hall that the hour of deliverance from oppression is near.

Dickens observes that "the comparison between the orator and the crowd of attentive faces turned toward him, was extremely to his disadvantage. ... He was not so honest, he was not so manly, he was not so good-humored; he substituted cunning for their simplicity, and passion for their safe and solid sense."

Yet the crowd of workers is most attentive, as if "every man felt his only hope to be in allying himself to the comrades by whom he was surrounded." These men were deluded in this belief, but they did not go "astray wholly without cause, and of their own irrational wills."

Comment

Dickens' account of the union meeting is crudely farcical in tone. He obviously loves the workers, but distrusts the demagoguery of the labor organizer. It has been suggested that he added this bit of anti-unionism to the novel to counteract the charges of being too anti-management.

Slackbridge, the union organizer, continues his harangue by announcing that there is one worker in their midst who will not join them in their "gallant stand for Freedom and for Right." It is Stephen Blackpool. The workers demand that he be given the chance to explain his stand.

Stephen tells the assembled workers very simply that he knows he is the only one not to join, but that he feels the union will do no good, only hurt to their cause. Besides, he has another reason, a private one, for not joining them. He realizes that his refusal will mean that all will shun him as the rules dictate, but he hopes that he will at least be allowed by them to continue at his job.

The chairman implores Stephen to think again before he takes the step which will mean certain ostracism. Stephen says only, "I simply canno coom in. I mun go th' ways as lays afore me." Then he leaves the hall.

"Thus easily," writes Dickens, "did Stephen Blackpool fall into the loneliest of lives, the life of solitude among a familiar crowd." The workers avoided him by general consent; "they even avoided that side of the street on which he habitually walked." He does not see Rachael for fear that she too would be shunned if she is seen with him.

One day "a young man of a very light complexion" stops him on the street to tell him that Bounderby wants to speak to him. He is to come to his employer's house.

Comment

The troubles of Stephen Blackpool strain the reader's credulity somewhat. His poorly motivated (in public at least) refusal to join the union and his immediate shunning by the workers who had all such a high opinion of him seem far-fetched. The Stephen Blackpool subplot is in general the weakest part of the book.

BRIGHT NOTES STUDY GUIDE

CHAPTER 5: MEN AND MASTERS

Stephen enters Bounderby's house to find not only his employer but Harthouse, Tom Gradgrind, and Louisa present as well. Bounderby curtly orders Stephen to speak up, to tell him about his trouble with the union.

Stephen, who has been suffering from the shunning by his fellow workers, resents the tone of Bounderby's address, for "it seemed to assume that he really was the self-interested deserter he had been called." He replies simply that he has nothing to say about it.

Bounderby turns to Harthouse and remarks about Stephen that "although they have put their mark upon him, he is such a slave to them still, that he's afraid to open his lips about them." Stephen interjects that he is not afraid to speak, but that he just does not wish to.

Stephen adds that he is sorry that the people have bad leaders, but that they can get no better. Bounderby is getting more and more angry at Stephen's quiet refusal to commit himself. He wants to know why Stephen would not join the union. Stephen, not wishing to be completely obstinate, admits at last that he had made a promise not to join.

Bounderby lets loose a windy tirade against the "set of rascals and rebels whom transportation [to the penal colonies] is too good for." How can Stephen defend them?

But Stephen does defend them. They are not rebels and rascals. They are true to one another, faithful and tender toward those in need. The people are patient and want to do what is right. The fault is not always with them.

Bounderby gets still more exasperated. He tells Harthouse, "the Parliament gentleman," to listen to the subversive talk of a worker in person. Stephen quietly points out that things are a muddle and that the shipping off to the penal settlements of "a hundred Slackbridges" would leave "the muddle just wheer 'tis." Instead of parliamentary investigations and statistical reports, dealing with the workers as human beings is the solution.

Comment

The long and confused sociological debate between Bounderby and Stephen Blackpool is one of the least successful parts of the novel. In his two debaters Dickens symbolizes the two contending classes, the capitalist and the worker. If Bounderby may be representative of predatory capitalism, Stephen Blackpool certainly is not a typical worker. His vague humanitarian views are representative of no one but himself (and of Dickens).

Stephen ends by saying that what the workers resent most of all is being rated and regulated "as if they was figures in a soom [sum], or machines; wi'out loves and likens, wi'out memories and inclinations, wi'out souls to weary and souls to hope. ..."

At this, Bounderby, red in face, blows up and accuses Stephen of being "such a waspish, raspish, ill-conditioned chap" that even his own fellow workers will have nothing to do with him. "I never thought those fellows could be right in anything," he adds, "... I'll have nothing to do with you either." Stephen is fired with these words, and with a "Heaven help us all in this world!" he departs.

CHAPTER 6: FADING AWAY

When Stephen steps out of Bounderby's house he meets Rachael and the mysterious old woman he had met at his last visit to his employer's. The old lady explains that she is on her annual visit to Coketown again and has met Rachael on the way. She has heard that Bounderby has married, and she has been lurking about the house to get a glimpse of his wife. Dickens hints that the old woman dwelt on the wedding with "strange enthusiasm."

Stephen assures her that Mrs. Bounderby is a fine young lady with dark eyes "and a still way." The old woman adds, "And what a happy wife!" Stephen, with a doubtful glance at Rachael, says that he supposes she is happy.

Stephen soon tells Rachael that he has lost his job at Bounderby's mill. It is just as well, for it would have brought trouble had he remained. He will leave Coketown to seek work elsewhere.

Stephen has overcome his initial vague dislike of the old woman. She is so contented, so sprightly, that he and Rachael befriend her and invite her to join them for a cup of tea at Stephen's place. As they approach his house, he glances at the window for fear his wife might have returned. But, adds Dickens, "the evil spirit of his life had flitted away again, months ago, and he had heard no more of her since."

When they are enjoying their tea and some fresh, buttered bread, the old lady reveals her name to be "Mrs. Pegler." She has been a widow for many years, she tells them, but when Stephen asks if there are any children she becomes nervous. At last she admits that she had a son, but "he is not to be spoken of. ... I have lost him."

The landlady comes to whisper in Stephen's ear that a visitor, a Mrs. Bounderby, is below. Mrs. Pegler, catching only "Bounderby," becomes panic-stricken. "Oh hide me! Don't let me be seen for the world," she cries. Stephen quiets the old woman by telling her that it is Mrs., not Mr., Bounderby who is coming up.

Comment

The mystification over the old woman continues. Her interest in Bounderby plus her fear of being seen by him, her pride in his achievements plus her story of having a son "lost" to her, should add up in the reader's mind to a strong suspicion as to who she is.

Louisa enters, accompanied by her brother Tom. Dickens comments that this is the first time she had ever been in the home of one of the Coketown workers. "She knew them in crowds passing to and from their nests, like ants or beetles. But she knew from her reading infinitely more of the ways of the toiling insects than of these toiling men and women." She had known the workers only as statistics in labor, crime, and pauperism, never as individual people.

She tells Stephen that she has come to help him in view of what she has witnessed at Bounderby's house. She asks Stephen if it is true that, fired by Bounderby, he can get no work anywhere else in Coketown. When she hears that it is so, she asks, "Then, by the prejudices of his own class, and by the prejudice of the other, he is sacrificed alike? Are the two so deeply separated in this town, that there is no place whatever, for an honest workman between them?" She tries to give Stephen some money, but he agrees to accept only a few pounds as a loan.

BRIGHT NOTES STUDY GUIDE

Comment

Louisa is beginning her education in earnest now. She has come to realize that people are more than mere automatons, that individuals may be crushed beneath contending ideas. By coming here to help Stephen, she is also beginning her revolt against her husband.

Tom has been so far a silent witness to these discussions. When they are ready to leave, he takes Stephen aside and tells him to appear outside the Bank after work. He should just loiter there for an hour or two each night until Tom can get him a certain message which will do him a good turn. He hints that he may be able to get a job for him.

After the old woman has been dropped off at the place where she will spend the night, Stephen says goodbye to Rachael. He promises to write her after he has left town. It is a heartfelt parting. Dickens adds an ominous warning: "Utilitarian economists, skeletons of schoolmasters, Commissioners of Fact, genteel and used-up infidels, gabblers of many little dog-eared creeds, the poor you will have always with you. Cultivate in them, while there is yet time, the utmost graces of the fancies and affections, to adorn their lives so much in need of ornament; or, in the day of your triumph, when romance is utterly driven out of their souls, and they and a bare existence stand face to face, Reality will take a wolfish turn, and make an end of you."

Comment

Here Dickens climbs upon his soapbox to deliver a polemic to the smug Victorian ruling class. If you do not preserve the humanity of the lower classes, they will someday rise and destroy you.

HARD TIMES

The next evening Stephen keeps his vigil outside Bounderby's Bank, and the next, and the next; nothing happens. No one comes with a message, and "Stephen even began to have an uncomfortable sensation upon him of being for the time a disreputable character."

Feeling that nothing has come of Tom's promise, he takes his few belongings early the next morning and leaves Coketown. It is pleasant for a change to trudge in the dirt of a country road instead of in the coal dust of the streets.

Comment

Tom's strange request of Stephen sets up a new situation. We know enough of Tom by now to understand that he is not motivated by pity for Stephen, but means to use him for some selfish purpose of his own. Dickens again ends a chapter on a note of suspense. The failure of Tom's message to come to Stephen only deepens it.

HARD TIMES

TEXTUAL ANALYSIS

BOOK 2: REAPING, CHAPTERS 7-12

CHAPTER 7: GUNPOWDER

Mr. Harthouse has been making good headway in Coketown politics because of his open opportunism and ability to compromise. "The not being troubled with earnestness was a grand point in his favor ...," writes Dickens.

He is holding forth to Louisa on his philosophy, or the lack of it. Virtue, benevolence, or philanthropy are all meaningless, he says. Her careful training in Gradgrindism had disposed her to agree with this view, but there was now also "a struggling disposition to believe in a wide and nobler humanity. ..." Her inward turmoil is eased by Harthouse's bland assumption that nothing really matters. She is slowly being drawn to him. As to Harthouse himself, "no energetic wickedness ruffled his lassitude." He toys with the idea of being the one whose presence brings joy and light to Louisa's face as her brothers does.

Comment

Dickens has prepared the ground for the seduction of Louisa by Harthouse. She is bored by her loveless marriage, and is unconsciously in revolt against it. She succumbs because she has no inner emotional resources to resist with.

The Bounderbys have moved to a large house about fifteen miles from town, the property of a bankrupt magnate. Bounderby with smug satisfaction takes over the estate and begins "with demonstrative humility to grow cabbages in the flower garden." He sneers at the elegant furniture and expensive artworks, and tells people he had lived on garbage and slept in market baskets when a boy.

One evening Harthouse comes upon Louisa sitting alone in the garden. He tells her that he has an interest in her brother. Tom has taken to gambling and is seriously in debt, he tells her. Louisa reluctantly admits that she has been giving Tom money for some time. She is worried over him. Harthouse magnanimously promises to be a good influence on Tom and to extricate him from his troubles. (Actually there is a strong hint that Harthouse has been encouraging Tom to live high.)

Tom appears and is in a rather sulky mood. After Louisa leaves, he and Harthouse wander in the garden. Tom admits that he is terribly in debt and upbraids his sister for not giving him more money. She married old Bounderby for his sake, he tells Harthouse, "then why doesn't she get what I want, out of him, for my sake?" Even the cynical Harthouse is disgusted by this heartless selfishness. He offers to lend Tom the money, but Tom, in tears now, says it is too late. But he will never forget what a true friend Mr. Harthouse is.

Harthouse is gratified later that evening to see that Louisa has a smile for him too now, that Tom is no longer the only creature she cares for.

Comment

Harthouse has gotten through to Louisa by playing on her love for her worthless brother, by posing as Tom's benefactor. Dickens, in having Tom involved in gambling debts to the point of tears, is preparing the reader for the events of the next few chapters.

CHAPTER 8: EXPLOSION

The next morning Mr. Harthouse sits in the bay window of his dressing room, smoking his rare tobacco in an Eastern pipe and reflecting upon his success with Louisa Bounderby. "He had established a confidence with her, from which her husband was excluded," writes Dickens, "... a confidence ... that absolutely turned upon her indifference toward her husband ... and the barrier behind which she lived, had melted away." He still had no "any earnest wickedness of purpose in him," but let himself drift. "The end to which it led was before him, pretty plainly; but he troubled himself with no calculations about it. What will be, will be."

When later in the day he comes to Bounderby's house, the banker shouts to him that the Bank has been robbed. It was robbed the previous night, entry having been gained by a false key. Only a small sum, 150 pounds, was taken from a small safe in Tom's office, fortunately. He adds that when Louisa heard of the robbery she "dropped, sir, as if she was shot. ..."

Comment

The discerning reader can guess from the various clues that Tom must have had something to do with the robbery. At least his sister thinks so.

Bitzer and Mrs. Sparsit join them and add their bit to the news of the robbery. Bitzer, as usual, had slept on his cot before the main vault. Tom had locked the stolen sum in his safe as always. During the night someone with a false key, which was later found in the street, opened the Bank and took the money from Tom's safe. When Harthouse asks if anyone is being suspected of the robbery, he is told that it is one of the hands, Stephen Blackpool to be exact. "Show me a dissatisfied Hand, and I'll show you a man that's fit for anything bad, I don't care what it is," adds Bounderby. Stephen was seen, he tells Harthouse, lurking about the Bank for several nights before the robbery. Mrs. Sparsit had noticed him and even pointed him out to Bitzer. An old woman was seen watching the place too. Now both of them are gone from Coketown. But they will be apprehended, he is sure. Harthouse comments, "Fellows who go in for Banks must take the consequences. If there were no consequences, we should all go in for Banks."

Comment

Dickens makes it plain to the reader that Stephen Blackpool has been framed to giving the appearance of a suspect in the robbery. It was Tom who set him up for this. If there is any lingering doubt over his guilt, this should clear it up. The accidental involvement of the old woman (Mrs. Pegler) as a suspect will also have important consequences. The search for her and her eventual unmasking will have a great effect on the affairs of both Bounderby and Mrs. Sparsit. This is a good example of the way Dickens prepares future plot developments far in advance.

Because Mrs. Sparsit's nerves have been badly jangled by the robbery, Bounderby invites her to stay for a few days at his house. She behaves in her usual manner, mixing self-abasing humility with reminders of her former high station. She constantly (but with coy apologies) refuses to call Louisa Mrs. Bounderby, referring to her as Miss Gradgrind still. She plays Backgammon with Bounderby, who always found the game relaxing, and she obtrusively reminds him that Louisa never liked it. She makes him his favorite drink, warm sherry with lemon peel and nutmeg, something Louisa doesn't do. In short she works hard to show him how much he has missed by losing her ministrations to his comfort by marriage to Louisa.

Comment

Mrs. Sparsit's attitude toward Mr. Bounderby is still ambiguous. Is she trying to show him that he made a mistake in marrying Louisa and should have married her?

Louisa nervously awaits the return of Tom. Soon after midnight, when he has returned, she noiselessly steals to his room. She kneels beside his bed in the dark and says to him, "Tom, have you anything to tell me? If ever you loved me in your life, and have anything concealed from everyone besides, tell it to me?"

He steadfastly denies that he has anything to tell her. He is concealing nothing. He suggests that she should say nothing about their visit to Stephen's lodgings. He tells her that when he took Stephen aside, he had merely told him to accept Louisa's money and make good use of it. He has nothing further to say.

Louisa leaves him, and when she is gone he bursts into tears, "... impenitently spurning himself, and no less hatefully and unprofitably spurning all the good in the world."

Comment

Tom is now revealed as a thorough cad. His sister gives him the opportunity to confess, but not only does he refuse, he adds insult to injury by further implicating an innocent man, Stephen Blackpool.

CHAPTER 9: HEARING THE LAST OF IT

Mrs. Sparsit, recovering her nerves in Mr. Bounderby's house, entertains herself by watching everything and everybody from "under her Coriolanian eyebrows," and prowling about. She cultivates the acquaintance of Harthouse, who returns the honor by making her compliments. She observes to him that of late, Miss Gradgrind (as she calls Louisa) seems more animated than usual.

At breakfast she solicitously makes Bounderby's tea, pointing out that Louisa is not there to do it. When Louisa enters, she relinquishes her job as hostess with a great show of pity, as if to imply that Louisa would do it only reluctantly. This provokes Bounderby. He says that for Louisa his will is also law, that if she offends him he would say so right out. The breakfast ends in a strained atmosphere. Dickens points out that from then on "the Sparsit action upon Mr. Bounderby threw Louisa and James Harthouse more together, and strengthened the dangerous alienation from her husband." Mrs. Sparsit after breakfast plants a kiss upon Mr. Bounderby's hand and murmurs, "My benefactor!" But later, she looks up at his portrait on the wall, makes "a contemptuous grimace at that work of art," and says, "Serve you right, you Noodle, and I am glad of it."

Comment

Mrs. Sparsit is aware of the rift between Bounderby and Louisa (has indeed helped it along) and welcomes the coming break-up of their marriage.

Bitzer, the colorless light porter, appears with a note from Stone Lodge, the Gradgrind residence. Mrs. Gradgrind is at death's door and wants to see Louisa. Since her marriage, Louisa has seldom been back in her old home. Her father was usually away in London at Parliament, her mother perpetually on her sofa didn't want visitors, her young brothers and sister she felt herself unfit for, and toward Sissy she had never again softened. "She had no inducements to go back, and had rarely gone," writes Dickens. "Her remembrances of home and childhood were remembrances of the drying up of every spring and fountain in her young heart as it gushed out."

She enters the house to find her mother with Sissy, and Jane, her now ten-year-old sister beside her. Mrs. Gradgrind tells Louisa that her father had always seen to it that she and her brother learned all the sciences. But there was something, not an "Ology" or science, that he had missed or forgotten. She has often thought about it, but doesn't know what it is. She wants to write to him to find out. Louisa hands her a pen, but soon she drops it, for "the light that had always been feeble and dim behind the weak transparency, went out." She is dead.

Comment

The death of the vegetable-like Mrs. Gradgrind leaves us undisturbed. Although she supplied a faint note of humor mingled with pathos to the cast of characters, she was never much more than a voice whining that she would never hear the end of it.

CHAPTER 10: MRS. SPARSIT'S STAIRCASE

As Mrs. Sparsit's nerves recover but slowly, her stay at Bounderby's house drags out to several weeks. "Conscious of her altered station, she resigned herself with noble fortitude" to living there. She continues to show pity for Bounderby in his presence, but his portrait she continues to address contemptuously as that of a Noodle. Bounderby appreciates Mrs. Sparsit's perception of him as an abused man, and as he senses that Louisa objects to her presence, he invites the widow to return for weekend stays.

Mrs. Sparsit looks with relish upon these added opportunities to keep her piercing black eyes on Louisa. In her mind, Louisa stands upon a gigantic staircase "with a dark pit of shame and ruin at the bottom; and down those stairs, from day to day, hour to hour, she saw Louisa coming."

Comment

Mrs. Sparsit desires to be able to prove to Bounderby that his marriage to Louisa was wrong. She now suspects an affair with Harthouse going on. She is spying on the couple for the final evidence of Louisa's descent into the "pit of shame" at the bottom of the allegorical staircase.

Bounderby tells Mrs. Sparsit that nothing further has been heard of the suspects in the bank robbery. Neither Stephen Blackpool nor the mysterious old woman, his accomplice, has turned up.

That evening, while Mrs. Sparsit is packing up to return to her bank lodgings, she sees Louisa and Harthouse sitting in the garden. She notices that their heads are almost touching (Louisa is getting closer to the bottom of the staircase), but she cannot hear what they are saying. Harthouse is telling Louisa that he had thought right away that Stephen was a hypocrite. He professed morality and talked well, but like most who do these things, was ready to help himself to what he could get a hold of. Mr. Bounderby had provoked him by his gruff handling, and Stephen went out to rob the Bank, which deed "relieved his mind extremely." This simple, if cynical, analysis of Stephen's character seems to find agreement in Louisa, especially when Harthouse tells her that it is Tom's view also.

Mrs. Sparsit keeps watching Louisa and Harthouse, gathering news of them even when she is not there. "She kept her black eyes wide open, with no touch of pity, with no touch of compunction, all absorbed in interest." She is obsessed with the image of Louisa's descent down the staircase to adultery. But in spite of her "deference for Mr. Bounderby as contradistinguished from his portrait, Mrs. Sparsit had not the smallest interest of interrupting the descent. Eager to see it accomplished, and yet patient, she waited for the last fall, as for the ripeness and fulness of the harvest of her hopes."

CHAPTER 11: LOWER AND LOWER

Mr. Gradgrind briefly returns from his parliamentary affairs in London for his wife's funeral. (He "buried her in a businesslike manner," comments Dickens.)

In the meantime Mrs. Sparsit keeps watching her allegorical staircase. She spies on Louisa through her husband, her brother, Mr. Harthouse, through looking at letters, "through everything animate and inanimate that at any time went near the stairs."

One Friday Mr. Bounderby is called away for a three- or four-day business trip. He tells Mrs. Sparsit to spend her usual weekend at his place. When she suggests that Louisa might not agree with his invitation, he gruffly tells her that his word is enough. When he has left, Mrs. Sparsit invites Tom to share a lamb chop and some India ale with her. She pumps him as to Harthouse's whereabouts. She is told that the gentleman is in Yorkshire, hunting, but that he is due to return tomorrow. Tom adds that he wouldn't be surprised if he should happen to "stray" out to the Bounderbys' place. Mrs. Sparsit then asks him to relay a message to Louisa that she would not come out that weekend.

Comment

Mrs. Sparsit is taking advantage of Bounderby's absence to set a trap for Louisa which will tumble her into the pit at the bottom of the moral staircase. She suspects that Harthouse will go out to see Louisa, and that the lovers, thinking she will not be there, will be indiscreet. Tom, through his greed for free chops and ale, has again provided an enemy with ammunition against his sister.

On Saturday evening Mrs. Sparsit lurks outside the railway station where Tom is waiting for Harthouse to return from Yorkshire. The train arrives, but no Harthouse is on it. "This is a device to keep him out of the way," says Mrs. Sparsit, "Harthouse is with his sister now." Quickly she takes the train to the country house, arrives, hurries down the lane to the house just as night falls. She sneaks about the house to find her quarry, but it is dark and silent. She then looks for the lovers in the garden. At last she spies them through the gloom. Harthouse must have come secretly over the fields on horseback, for she sees his horse tied nearby.

She hears Harthouse say to Louisa, "Knowing you were alone, was it possible I should stay away?" Louisa tells Harthouse to leave her. He pleads, professes his love, his willingness to risk ruin for her sake, and he bemoans her coldness toward him. Mrs. Sparsit greedily takes in the lovemaking (but overlooks Louisa's reluctance), and when the lovers part because it is beginning to rain, she has the distinct impression that they had agreed to meet again that night. Although she is soaked by the now heavy rain, she keeps to her hiding place in the shrubbery even after Harthouse has ridden off and Louisa returned to the house. Mrs. Sparsit soon sees Louisa leave the house again, cloaked and muffled. She thinks to herself, "She elopes! She falls from the lower-most stair-, and is swallowed up in the gulf." She follows Louisa to the railroad station and enters the train with her, unseen. She must be on her way to Coketown, she surmises. When the train arrives, the rain has become a thunderous downpour. Mrs. Sparsit waits to see which carriage Louisa will take to meet her lover. To her chagrin no Louisa appears outside the station. She must have gotten off at some station before Coketown. "I have lost her!" Mrs. Sparsit groans amid tears of bitter frustration.

Comment

The pursuit of Louisa by Mrs. Sparsit is one of the best-written parts of *Hard Times*. Dickens exactly matches the moods of the characters with that of nature. The tension in Mrs. Sparsit mounts as she believes herself about to witness the elopement of Louisa and Harthouse. Parallel to this is the rain, which rises from a gentle patter to a torrential downpour with thunder and lightning. We will see that a similar storm took place in Louisa's heart simultaneously.

CHAPTER 12: DOWN

Mr. Gradgrind is home on vacation from his parliamentary duties. He is sitting in his study writing, only occasionally distracted by the sound of the rain and the peal of the thunder. Suddenly the door opens and Louisa, soaked and disheveled, appears. He asks her what has brought her to him in this storm. She asks in return, "Father, you have trained me from my cradle?" "Yes, Louisa," he replies. Then she says, "I curse the hour in which I was born to such a destiny." She goes on to remind him of the last talk they had had in this same room. "What has risen to my lips now, would have risen to my lips then, if you had given me a moment's help," she tells him. She asks him. "If you had known that there lingered in my breast, sensibilities, affections, weaknesses capable of being cherished into strength, defying all the calculations ever made by man, and no more known to his arithmetic than his Creator is, - would you have given me to the husband whom I am now sure that I hate?" He answers, "No. No, my poor child."

Comment

Like the thunderbolts in the storm outside, the unleashed passions of Louisa shatter the quiet statistical world of Gradgrind. He has thought that his educational system would protect her against all "fancies," against sentiments, and passions. He had never realized that she was more than an empty pitcher to be poured full of facts.

She continues her bitter reproaches to him. She had always had "an ardent impulse toward some region where rules and figures, and definitions were not quite absolute," but she had allowed him to suppress it. In her deadened state of mind she accepted Bounderby as her husband. She says, "I never made a pretense to him or you that I loved him." She made the best of it for Tom's sake. Then there came into her life another man, one "used to the world; light, polished, easy," who gained her confidence because he understood her relation to her husband. She tells her father that tonight the man had declared himself her lover, and is now expecting her to meet him. What is she to do, she cries. "All that I know is, your philosophy and your teaching will not save me." She sinks in a faint upon the floor, and Mr. Gradgrind sees "the pride of his heart, and the triumph of his system lying, an insensible heap, at his feet."

Comment

Just as the final chapter of Book 1 sees Gradgrind and Bounderby at the height of their triumph, their system victorious, their way of life supreme, so this chapter sees both men bitterly defeated.

HARD TIMES

TEXTUAL ANALYSIS

BOOK 3: GARNERING

CHAPTER 1: ANOTHER THING NEEDFUL

Louisa awakes in her old bed at home in her old room. Her little sister tells her that it was Sissy who had put her there, tended her, and who had made the room so cheerful. Louisa notices that her sister's face is beaming, so unlike her own when she had been her age. "I'm sure it must be Sissy's doing," her sister tells her in explanation.

Her father enters and tenderly asks how she is. "He spoke in a subdued and troubled voice, very different from his usual dictatorial manner, and was often at a loss for words," writes Dickens. He had proved his system to himself, he tells her, and "must bear the responsibility of its failures." He had always meant to do right. Now he mistrusts himself, feels unfit to guide her in her troubles. He realizes now that "there is a wisdom of the Head, and that there is a wisdom of the Heart." He has always thought that of the Head all-sufficient. It may not be.

Since he has spent so much time away from home lately, a new spirit has been in it. He has noted it in the younger children, even though they have been getting the same education as before. "Louisa, I have a misgiving that some change may have been slowly working about me in this house, by mere love and gratitude...," he tells her. Then he leaves.

Sissy enters. At first Louisa is resentful that she should be seen in her distress. She pretends to be asleep, but she is touched with remorse when she notices that Sissy is weeping over her. Sissy pleads with Louisa to be allowed to be of help. Louisa tells her that she is so proud, hardened, confused, and unjust that Sissy should feel repelled. Sissy answers that she is not repelled, and at last Louisa breaks down. She puts her arms around Sissy and cries out, "Forgive me, pity me, help me! Have compassion on my great need, and let me lay this head of mine upon a loving heart!" Sissy answers, "Lay it here! Lay it here, my dear."

Comment

The events of this chapter are largely a recapitulation of the last scene in the last chapter, which ended Book 2. Mr. Gradgrind admits the bankruptcy of his system and that the Heart has its wisdom. The transforming power of Sissy, the exponent of Heart-wisdom, begins to manifest itself. Finally, Louisa, in throwing herself upon the sympathy of Sissy, is asking Heart-wisdom to solve her troubles too.

CHAPTER 2: VERY RIDICULOUS

Mr. James Harthouse waits in the meanwhile for his appointment with Louisa. He is disturbed when she does not appear, more disturbed when no message from her comes, and most disturbed to find that she is neither at Bounderby's country nor town house. He goes to the Bank only to find that Mrs. Sparsit is gone too. Tom is there, annoyed at having been left waiting at the station in vain, but knowing nothing of his sister's whereabouts. Harthouse resigns himself to watchful waiting at his hotel, convinced that something has gone wrong and that a wrathful Bounderby will soon descend upon him.

Soon a waiter announces that a visitor is outside to see him, a young lady. He hurries out, finds not Louisa as he expected, but a young woman he has never seen before. It is Sissy, and she seems perfectly at ease, unafraid of him, and in no way disconcerted. She tells him that she comes from Louisa.

Harthouse is relieved at the news, but his momentary elation is dashed when he hears the rest of the message. Louisa is at her father's house, and will never see him again. When he presses Sissy for an explanation she repeats that he will never see Louisa again and is to entertain no hopes. All the while Harthouse is struck by the "child-like ingenuousness with which his visitor spoke, her modest fearlessness, her truthfulness which put all artifice aside. ..." He has never had experience with such a girl and is at a loss as to how to treat her.

Dickens writes that "he was touched in the cavity where his heart should have been. ..." "I am as immoral as need be," Harthouse tells Sissy. But he has no evil intentions toward Louisa and does not want to persecute her. Sissy asks him to leave Coketown to undo the harm he has done. He pleads that he has political obligations to fulfill. She insists that his leaving would be the only reparation in his power. After pledging her to secrecy to preserve his dignity, he agrees to her request.

After Sissy has left, he writes a letter to his highly placed brother that he is bored with Coketown affairs and will take up with camels. He sends a note to Bounderby announcing his retirement from the area, and is soon in a railway carriage, leaving the dark landscape behind him. He has a "secret sense of having failed and been ridiculous," but also the relief of having "escaped the **climax** of a very bad business."

Comment

The routing of the languid cynic, Mr. James Harthouse, by the ingenuous Sissy, while sentimentally satisfying, is not well motivated. That a Harthouse should give in so easily to Sissy's plea to end the affair, and on top of it to relinquish his career in Coketown, seems overdone. But in Dickens' world, the Heart always triumphs over the Head, even in villains.

CHAPTER 3: VERY DECIDED

Mrs. Sparsit, sneezing and hoarse from the cold she caught while spying on Louisa in the rain, rushes off to London to report her discovery to Bounderby. Finding him, and giving her report "with infinite relish," she then faints. Mr. Bounderby, after roughly restoring her to her senses, hustles her into a train and takes her back to Coketown. There he crams her into a coach and bears her off to Stone Lodge to confront Mr. Gradgrind as a witness to his daughter's defection.

Gradgrind is "surprised by the apparition," but asks Bounderby is he has received his letter about Louisa. Bounderby roars that he doesn't care about letters in his state of mind. He begins telling Gradgrind about Mrs. Sparsit's discovery, but

Gradgrind calmly replies that he knows the contents of the overheard conversation.

Bounderby demands to know where Louisa is. Gradgrind tells him that she is here, in her old home. He explains that just after the conversation which Mrs. Sparsit had overheard, Louisa had hurried home to her father for protection. Bounderby turns to Mrs. Sparsit and tells that wretched lady, "Now, ma'am. We shall be happy to hear any little apology you may think proper to offer, for going about the country at express pace, with no other luggage than a cock-and-a-bull, ma'am." Mrs. Sparsit replies that her nerves are too much shaken, and she collapses in tears.

Comment

Mrs. Sparsit, the officious meddler, has met defeat at last, even in the eyes of her employer. She thought she had proof of Louisa's elopement with Harthouse; now instead, Louisa is at her father's. She has made a fool of herself before Bounderby and, worse yet, has caused him to look foolish too.

Bounderby tells Gradgrind that he has not been "as dutifully and submissively treated" by Louisa "as Josiah Bounderby of Coketown ought to be treated by his wife." Gradgrind counters that both of them had made a mistake; they have not understood Louisa. He admits that her education has been wrong. There are qualities in Louisa "which have been harshly neglected - and a little perverted." He suggests that Louisa should be allowed to stay with him for a while to be attended by Sissy, "who understands her and in whom she trusts."

Bounderby, his face crimson and swollen, says, "I gather ... that you are of opinion that there's what people call some incompatibility between Loo Bounderby and myself." Her father sorrowfully admits that seems to be the case.

Bounderby launches a tirade on his favorite theme-imaginative qualities always mean that the person wants turtle-soup and venison with a gold spoon, and to ride in a coach-and-six. If that's what Louisa wants, Gradgrind will have to give it to her because he won't. The only incompatibility he sees is that Gradgrind's daughter "don't properly know her husband's merits, and is not impressed with such a sense as would become her, by George! of the honor of his alliance."

When Gradgrind states that his view is unreasonable, Bounderby suggests that there are "ladies-born ladies-belonging to families-Families!-who next to worship the ground" he walks on. Louisa is not such a born lady, and in the opinion of a certain born lady, has treated him rather shamefully.

Gradgrind wants to end this fruitless conversation, but Bounderby insists on settling things now. He lays down the ultimatum that "if she don't come home tomorrow, by twelve o'clock at noon, I shall understand that she prefers to stay away. ..." He will then send her things back to Gradgrind's house and her father will have to provide for her future. People will understand that it was she, not he, who would not come up to the mark.

After accusing Gradgrind of having succumbed to "sentimental humbug," Bounderby leaves for his town house. The next day, after the time for Louisa's return had expired, he sends her things over to Stone Lodge, puts his estate up for sale, and resumes a bachelor life.

HARD TIMES

Comment

Just as Mr. Gradgrind has met defeat (the failure of his educational system) in Louisa's return, so now Bounderby meets defeat with the realization that his wife will not come back to him. His only consolation seems to be that Mrs. Sparsit adores him, a slave for his wounded ego.

CHAPTER 4: LOST

Mr. Bounderby throws himself vigorously into his work to show the world that his domestic troubles bother him little. He also renews the search for the perpetrators of the Bank robbery by having placards printed offering a reward of twenty pounds for the apprehension of Stephen Blackpool. These placards, posted all over Coketown, cause a great stir, and are always surrounded by curious groups of workers.

Slackbridge, the union delegate, at a meeting displays the placard and reminds the workers how this same Stephen Blackpool, this traitor to their cause, had once argued with him. They had rightly cast him out, for he is now branded a thief, a plunderer, a "proscribed fugitive with a price upon his head." Slackbridge has the union pass a resolution (against very feeble opposition) that the workers of Coketown, having disowned Stephen Blackpool, are "free from the shame of his misdeeds, and cannot as a class be reproached with his dishonest actions."

Comment

The speech of Slackbridge at the meeting gives Dickens another opportunity of denouncing what he considers the hypocritical demagoguery of the labor organizer. Dickens is merely countering his recent exposure of a bad capitalist (Bounderby) with a reminder that callous and bombastic stupidity can be found in the other classes too.

The evening after the placards have appeared, Sissy announces to Louisa that Bounderby, her brother Tom, and a young woman named Rachael are there to see her. With Mr. Gradgrind present, they are admitted. Bounderby greets Louisa coolly, and tells Mr. Gradgrind that because his son has refused to comment about the statements the young woman made to him, it is necessary to confront her with Louisa. Tom, who entered with them, remains inconspicuously in the background during this explanation.

Rachael asks Louisa to state if she has seen her before, where it was, and who else was present. Tom coughs a signal, but Louisa promptly replies that it was at Stephen's place, the night after he had been fired, and that her brother Tom had been there as well as an old lady who hadn't spoken. At this, Bounderby wants to know of Tom why he hadn't given this information. Tom says that he had promised his sister that he wouldn't, and he bitterly adds that she tells the story so much better and fuller than he would.

Rachael next asks if it isn't so that Louisa offered Stephen a banknote, but that he had only accepted a few coins. Why had she done this? When Louisa says that she is sorry for Stephen, Rachael counters with, "I hope you maybe, but I don't know! I can't say what you may ha' done! The like of you don't know us, don't care for us, don't belong to us." She suggests that Louisa might have had an ulterior motive for coming that night and offering help.

Bounderby then steps in to remind Rachael of her other statement. She had said that she had written to Stephen and that he would be here in two days to clear his name. He does not believe her. She too has been under suspicion, her mail has been watched, and no letter to Stephen has gone out. When Rachael explains that Stephen has assumed another name, Bounderby takes this as further evidence of his guilt. Louisa hopes that Stephen will return and clear himself. When they leave, Tom has only a dark scowl for Louisa. Mr. Gradgrind asks Louisa if she is certain Stephen is innocent, and when she replies that she is, he muses, "I ask myself, does the real culprit know of these accusations? Where is he? Who is he?"

Sissy goes to Rachael's room each night to get news of Stephen's return. There is none, night after night, even after the two days are over. Tom, meanwhile grows "greatly excited, horribly fevered, bit his nails down to the quick, spoke in a hard rattling voice, and with lips that were black and burnt up." No Stephen arrives in Coketown, although it is known that he has left his last working place. He has simply vanished.

Comment

Dickens manages to build up considerable suspense in this chapter. Tom is about to be unmasked as the real criminal, a thing by now rather obvious to even the most obtuse reader. The reader can share his growing sense of fear, of the net closing in. Characteristically, Tom reproaches his sister for not covering up for him when confronted with Rachael's statement, instead of taking the blame himself. Another element of suspense is created when Stephen does not appear at the stated time.

CHAPTER 5: FOUND

Day after day passes, but no Stephen appears. Each night Sissy goes to Rachael's lodging to inquire after news. Rachael is in despair because so few people still believe in Stephen's innocence. She is buoyed up only by Sissy's confidence. "I get hope and strength through you," she tells her. Sissy comforts her by telling her that all at Stone Lodge are sure Stephen will be cleared someday. Rachael says that she regrets having suspected Louisa of sinister intentions, but she feels that someone would be confounded by Stephen's return and proven innocence. This person, she fears, may have murdered Stephen to prevent his return. Stephen could easily have walked the distance in two days, and he has not stopped off at any of the inns en route. She is worried. Sissy arranges with Rachael that on Sunday they will take a walk in the country to relax for the next week of work and waiting.

Comment

More suspense is being built up by the imputation that perhaps the real criminal, Tom, has done away with Stephen to protect himself. Is it possible that Tom is that bad?

Rachael is walking Sissy home when they pass Mr. Bounderby's town house. A carriage has just stopped there, and Mrs. Sparsit is alighting. She calls out to them, exclaiming that it must be Providence that has put them there at this very time. She drags out of the carriage the mysterious old woman, the supposed accomplice of Stephen Blackpool. Accompanied by Rachael and Sissy, and about twenty-five nosy neighbors, she hales the old woman before Mr. Bounderby who is there in the company of Mr. Gradgrind and Tom. Mrs. Sparsit proudly presents her quarry to her employer, telling him that she has gone through considerable trouble in finding the culprit, "but trouble in your service, is to me a pleasure, and hunger, thirst, and cold a real gratification."

Imagine her surprise when she notes that Mr. Bounderby's face reveals nothing but discomfiture at the sight of the old woman, Mrs. Pegler. "Why don't you mind your own business, ma'am?" he roars at Mrs. Sparsit. "How dare you go and poke your officious nose into my family affairs?"

"My dear Josiah!" cries Mrs. Pegler, "My darling boy!"

Comment

Mrs. Sparsit has committed her second and fatal blunder in her zeal to please Mr. Bounderby. She has confronted him with his own mother, so long denigrated and denied. Of course the reader has long suspected the old woman to be Bounderby's mother.

Mr. Gradgrind tells the old woman that she should be ashamed to face her son after her "unnatural and inhuman treatment" of him, having left him as an infant to the "brutality of a drunken grandmother." Mrs. Pegler replies that the grandmother had died before Josiah was even born, that he had not been brought up in a gutter, but that his parents had pinched to provide him with a good schooling. He had been apprenticed to a kind master, and worked his "way forward to be rich and thriving." Josiah had pensioned her under the condition that she not trouble him with her presence, nor talk about him at all. Once a year she had come to Coketown to see her darling boy and admire him from afar.

The bystanders murmur their sympathy for Mrs. Pegler, but Mr. Bounderby's head grows redder and more swollen. He disperses the crowd with the statement that he will offer no explanations of his family affairs. Dickens comments, "Detected as a bully of humility, who had built his windy reputation upon lies, and in his boastfulness had put the honest truth as far away from himself as if he had advanced the mean claim (there is no meaner) to tack himself on to a pedigree, he cut a most ridiculous figure."

Now that Mrs. Pegler was shown to have had no connection with the robbery, Stephen's innocence seems more certain. Louisa fears that Tom is the person who would be confounded by Stephen's reappearance, that he is the real thief.

Comment

The unmasking of Bounderby as a windy "bully of humility," who deliberately denigrated his own mother and his family background in order to build up his own ego, is morally satisfying. That his wife should leave him is humiliating enough, but that he should be exposed as a phony self-made man who did not rise from rags to riches on his own merits is worse. It must be admitted that the setting for this welcome event is theatrical, with not only all the main characters of the novel on hand, but an audience of bystanders as well. Coincidence has been stretched to the point of incredibility, but actually *Hard Times* suffers less from this common defect of nineteenth-century novels than the other works of Dickens.

CHAPTER 6: THE STARLIGHT

Sissy and Rachael meet early on Sunday to walk in the country as they had planned. Because the smoky factories have polluted the area around Coketown itself, they have to take the train a few miles out of town before they can find open, unspoiled country. Even here the marks of industry are still to be seen: occasional heaps of coal or slag, deserted works overgrown with weeds, patches of brambles surrounded by broken fences which denote the presence of abandoned mine shafts.

Passing one such fence, Sissy notices that it is freshly broken. She goes in a ways and comes upon a hat lying in the grass. Written inside is the owner's name: Stephen Blackpool. A few steps beyond is the "brink of a black ragged chasm hidden by the thick grass." Rachael screams out that he must be down there. They crawl to the edge of the pit and call his name. No answer comes from the depths of the shaft. They decide to run for help, and soon a group of workmen come with windlasses, ropes, and lanterns at the news that a man has fallen down the Old Hell Shaft.

Comment

The discovery of the pit into which Stephen may have fallen (or been thrown), one pit of many which dot the countryside, by the two girls who just happen upon it, is another of the overdone coincidences of *Hard Times*.

Hours later, the windlasses have been erected and the operation of bringing up the fallen man may begin. Bounderby, Gradgrind, Louisa and Tom have also made their appearance at the pit side by now. A man goes down, and coming back up, reports that Stephen is still alive, although fatally hurt. Stephen has told him that upon hearing that he was wanted, he had made his way toward Bounderby's country house. He had fallen into the mine shaft after dark, and had lain there ever since, keeping himself alive with some scraps of food he had in his pocket.

When at last the broken body of Stephen is brought up, he is barely able to call out the name of Rachael. The muddle will soon be over him, he tells her. That the pit should be his death is nothing, for it had cost the lives of hundreds of workers when it was in use. "When it were in work, it killed wi'out need; when 'tis let alone, it kills wi'out need. See how we die an' no need, one way an' another-in a muddle-every day!"

From the pit bottom, he tells her, he could see a star above. This star has cleared his muddled mind. He tells Mr. Gradgrind that his son can clear him, for he had spoken with him the night of the robbery. With Rachael holding his hand, he then dies. Says Dickens, "The star had shown him where to find the God of the Poor; and through humility, and sorrow, and forgiveness, he had gone to his Redeemer's rest."

Comment

The death of Stephen Blackpool is another contrived theatrical affair with a large and complete crowd of people present. At least the reader is relieved to discover that Stephen had fallen, in not been pushed.

CHAPTER 7: WHELP-HUNTING

When the ring of people around the Old Hell Shaft breaks up, Tom has disappeared. He is nowhere to be found. Gradgrind goes to Bounderby to tell him that Tom would not be in the office for a while, and that he would clear Stephen Blackpool and declare the real thief. Gradgrind spends much time in his study, pacing back and forth, lost in thought.

When he emerges, he seems more aged and bent than before, "yet he looked a wiser man, and a better man, than in the days when in this life he wanted nothing but Facts." He talks at last to Louisa about Tom. The robbery, he tells her, must have been planned when they went to Stephen's lodgings. Stephen's leaving town gave Tom the idea of casting suspicion on him by having him loiter around the bank before he left. It is all clear now.

The next problem is, how is Tom to be found, and by them alone? Sissy announces shyly that she has already arranged it. It was she who told Tom to flee at the pit shaft. He has been sent to Sleary's circus, to be hidden until she came. They arrange to go there by circuitous routes so as not to arouse suspicion. Perhaps Tom could be spirited out of the country.

Sissy and Louisa travel together, changing from train to train, and to coaches until they at last come upon Sleary's Horseriding. Kidderminster, now "too maturely turfy" to be an infant prodigy, is at the entrance booth, but he does not recognize them. Inside the tent, the show is going on and the acts seem endless to the girls who are so anxious to have Mr. Sleary tell them where Tom is hidden.

At last they are able to sit with Sleary in his private quarters. He first tells Sissy all the news of the circus, who has married whom, what new acts there are, and so on. The various members of the troupe come in and renew their acquaintance with Sissy. When Louisa asks for Tom, Sleary tells her to look at the ring through a peephole. In the act now in progress, Tom is one of the black servants. No one could recognize him, and after the performance the girls and Mr. Gradgrind (who has also arrived) can talk to Tom in private.

When at last they meet Tom, he is still dressed in a "preposterous coat, like a beadle's with cuffs and flaps exaggerated to an unspeakable extent," and he is still in blackface. Mr. Gradgrind could hardly believe that "one of his model children had come to this."

Comment

To heighten the effect, Dickens has Tom make his last appearance in the novel at the circus, for the reader had first met him there as a small boy, peeping inside. Remembering Gradgrind's consternation then, it is poetic justice that he should see Tom for the last time as a ludicrous circus performer.

Tom sulkily admits to his father that he has committed the robbery. That he had been dishonest is a matter of statistics, the law of averages catching up, he avers as a weak defense. Gradgrind tells him that he is to go abroad. Sleary will disguise him as a carter. All is in readiness soon. Tom says goodbye to his broken-hearted father, but for Louisa he has only reproaches. She betrayed him, he says, by telling people of their visit to Stephen.

Just as he is about to leave in his new disguise, Bitzer appears, "his colorless face more colourless than ever." He collars Tom and announces that he won't allow himself to be foiled by horseriders.

CHAPTER 8: PHILOSOPHICAL

Mr. Gradgrind appeals to Bitzer. "Have you a heart?" Yes, he has one, but is accessible only to Reason, to nothing else, he replies. He tells Gradgrind that he has suspected Tom from the start, and has been watching him very closely, and has followed them there. He will deliver Tom to Bounderby and justice in the expectation that he will be promoted to Tom's position.

Gradgrind states, that in other words, it is merely a matter of self-interest to Bitzer. The colorless young man replies that "the whole social system is a question of self-interest." This is what he has been taught in Gradgrind's own school. Bitzer refuses a bribe to let Tom go, for he has already calculated that his promotion would be more advantageous.

Writes Dickens, "It was a fundamental principle of the Gradgrind philosophy that everything was to be paid for. Nobody was ever on any account to give anybody anything, or render anybody help without purchase. Gratitude was to be abolished, and the virtues springing from it were not to be. Every inch of the existence of mankind, from birth to death, was to be a bargain across a counter. And if we didn't get to Heaven that way, it was not a politico-economical place, and we had no business there."

Comment

This is the final blow to the Gradgrind philosophy of practical self-interest. Bitzer, his prize pupil, brought up on the very principles he himself had preached, is now the means by which Tom will be denied a chance at freedom. The utilitarian chickens have come home to roost with a vengeance.

Sleary, professing sympathy with Bitzer's views, offers to drive them to the railway station. But it is only a ruse to allow Tom to escape. Sleary's trained dog keeps Bitzer at a bay until Tom has been safely gotten aboard a ship.

To the grateful Mr. Gradgrind, Sleary says that some time ago, Merrylegs, the performing dog of Sissy's father, had come back to the circus, and had then died. This is a certain sign that her father must be dead too, for the dog would never leave him. But he doesn't want Sissy to know. He philosophizes a bit over his brandy and water that there is love in the world too, not only self-interest. His parting word to Gradgrind is that he shouldn't be cross with poor vagabonds. People must be amused. They can't always be learning or working.

Comment

The loose ends of the novel are beginning to be tied up. Sissy's father has been accounted for, Bitzer has been foiled, Tom gotten to safety. It is strange that it occurs to no one that Tom is, after all, a thief, and deserves punishment.

CHAPTER 9: FINAL

Mr. Bounderby is "unappeasably indignant" with Mrs. Sparsit over her discovery of Mrs. Pegler, and he finally comes to the conclusion that to discharge her would give him the most satisfaction and her the most punishment. At lunch one day he tells Mrs. Sparsit of his displeasure with her. She must feel cramped under his humble roof, he hints; there is not enough scope for a lady with her "genius in other people's affairs." He suggests that her relative, Lady Scadgers, might have affairs that could be interfered with. She may take her time to leave, but he will apologize now for having stood in her light so long.

Instead of being shattered by her dismissal, Mrs. Sparsit is scornful. "Nothing that a Noodle does, can awaken surprise or indignation," she tells him. "The proceedings of a Noodle can only inspire contempt." Thus she sweeps majestically out of his life.

Comment

That this high-born lady, of whose adoration he had been so convinced, now reveals only contempt for him, is a final blow to Bounderby's ego. Even the mean little victory of hurting her by discharging her was not to be his.

What of the future of all these people, asks Dickens? Could Bounderby know that within five years he was to die in a fit on a Coketown street and his estate subjected to a long career of fraudulent litigation? Did Gradgrind see himself as a white-haired decrepit man, disowned by his party for "bending his hitherto inflexible theories to appointed circumstances; making his facts and figures subservient to Faith, Hope, and Charity; and no longer trying to grind that Heavenly trio in his dusty little mills"?

What of Louisa's future? She was never to have a husband again, or have children of her own, except that Sissy's happy children were close to her. Louisa was fated to spend her life "trying hard to know her humbler fellow creatures, and to beautify their lives of machinery and reality.........." Her brother Tom, thousands of miles away, often wrote to her on paper blotted with tears of his wish to see her once again. It was never to be, for he died before he ever could. His last word was her name.

Rachael was to resume her old way of life after a long illness, and could be seen often taking care of a drunken derelict of a woman, the wife of the dead Stephen Blackpool.

Comment

True to the tradition of the nineteenth-century novel, Dickens ends by letting the reader know what becomes of the various characters later on.

The ending of *Hard Times* is a downbeat one, a series of negatives, rather than the usual Dickensian positives. Gradgrind has lost a theory, Bounderby a wife and an adoring housekeeper, Mrs. Sparsit a position, Louisa her future as a rich man's wife, Rachael a friend, and Stephen Blackpool his life. The only thing that remains unchanged is Sleary's circus.

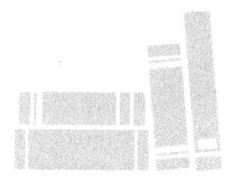

HARD TIMES

CHARACTER ANALYSES

Hard Times is remarkable among the novels of Dickens not only for its brevity, but for its small cast of characters. In contrast to the *Pickwick Papers*, in which there are about three hundred and fifty characters, or to *David Copperfield*, in which some forty characters play some role, in *Hard Times* there are only seventeen people who have a part of any significance. They are listed in alphabetical order.

BITZER

A living proof of the effect of Gradgrindism on people. He is colorless, light-eyed, light-haired, light-complexioned - as if all his color had been drawn out - and he becomes the light porter in Bounderby's Bank. An apt pupil of the utilitarian philosophy of self-interest, he subordinates human feelings to his ambitions.

STEPHEN BLACKPOOL

A forty-year-old power-loom weaver in Bounderby's mill. Sober, industrious, and of great personal integrity, he refuses to join the labor union. Ostracized by his fellow workers, he yet defends their union rights toward Bounderby, who then fires and blacklists him. He is married to an alcoholic wife who has deserted him, and is in love with Rachael, a working woman. His sense of personal honor keeps his relationship with Rachaep chaste, and his inability to rid himself legally of his derelict wife is one of the social abuses castigated by Dickens in the novel. Stephen dies after falling into an abandoned mine shaft on the way back to clear his name after having been unjustly accused of robbery.

MRS. BLACKPOOL

The drunken derelict wife of Stephen. She had been a friend of Rachael's when both were girls together in the mills. Married to Stephen, she became an alcoholic and left him after selling off the household goods for drink. She occasionally returns to him to help and to torment him. Both Stephen and Rachael are generous toward her although she is preventing their happiness together.

JOSIAH BOUNDERBY

Banker, mill-owner, and chief villain in *Hard Times*. Fifty years old, "a big, loud man, with a stare, and a metallic laugh ... a man made out of a coarse material ... with a great puffed head and forehead, swelled veins in his temples. ..." He is a braggart, a "bully of humility," whose constant boast is that he has worked his way up to power and wealth from the lowliest beginnings, ignorance, and poverty. He is vulgar, ostentatious, and brutally callous of the feelings of others. One of the most satisfying parts of the novel is his unmasking as a fraud who had actually come of respectable parents, been educated, and given a proper start in life.

THOMAS GRADGRIND SR.

Father of Louisa and Tom, he is a businessman who later becomes a Member of Parliament. Chief exponent of utilitarianism, of the absolute dominance of facts over feelings, he represents the doctrinaire approach to life. Everything about his appearance is square, from his forehead to his fingers. His children he brings up well taught in the sciences, but deprived of parental affection and common humanity. A good man at heart, he is gradually brought back to his own humanity by the troubles his theories have brought upon his children, and by the influence of Sissy Jupe, who represents the triumph of heart over head.

MRS. GRADGRIND

"... a little, thin, white, pink-eyed bundle of shawls, of surpassing feebleness, mental and bodily; who was always taking physic without any effect, and who, whenever she showed a symptom of coming to life, was invariably stunned by some weighty piece of fact tumbling on her." Loveless toward her children, ineffectual mother in a loveless household, married to Gradgrind in a marriage of arrangement, she represents the dominated Victorian wife at her weakest. When she dies, there are few tears.

LOUISA GRADGRIND (MRS. BOUNDERBY)

Although subjected to utilitarian education from childhood, she is inwardly rebellious, and given to moments of forbidden daydreaming. She regards only her brother Tom with affection, and for his sake marries the odious Mr. Bounderby, a man thirty years her senior, whom she does not love. She grows increasingly rebellious against her loveless marriage and the futility of her life by befriending the fired Stephen Blackpool, by allowing Mr. Harthouse to court her, and at last by leaving her husband to return to her father. The break-up of her marriage and her reproaches to her father for having ruined her life with his false doctrines cause a change of heart in him.

THOMAS GRADGRIND JR.

Louisa's brother, a selfish egoist who exploits his sister's affection for him for his own ends and to her ruin. He is another product of the philosophy of facts and self-interest; a coward who doesn't rebel against his father although he hates the system, a sycophant who fawns upon the upper-class James Harthouse and practically throws his sister in his way as a mistress, and finally, a sneak thief who robs Bounderby and arranges to have the innocent Stephen Blackpool suspected of the crime. Unregenerate, even at the end after being caught and barely saved from well-deserved justice, he blames only his sister because she would not cover up his crime.

JAMES HARTHOUSE, ESQUIRE

An effete young man of aristocratic family who is sent to Coketown to enter politics on behalf of the Gradgrind party. He is languid, cynical, bored with everything, and devoid of both ideals and ideas. He carries on a flirtation with Louisa to ease his boredom. About to elope with her, he is persuaded by Sissy to give her up, a rare act of idealism on his part.

MR. JUPE

Father of Sissy Jupe, he is a clown and performer in Sleary's Horseriding, a traveling circus. He is a widower, and devoted to his only daughter, whom he puts into Gradgrind's school to be educated for a better life. As he is no longer skillful at his trade and has taken to drink in frustration, he abandons Sissy in order to enable her to have a more secure life. When his performing dog, Merrylegs, returns to the circus alone at the novel's end, we know he must have died.

CECILIA (SISSY) JUPE

A dark-eyed, dark-haired girl, daughter of a strolling circus performer, she is enrolled in Gradgrind's school, but is not an apt pupil for the hard-facts educational theory. An affectionate, imaginative girl, she represents the world of feeling, of heart over head. Her presence in the Gradgrind household after her father's desertion gradually affects those about her for the better. She acts as a catalytic agent, precipitating a reaction against the inherent inhumanism of the Gradgrind philosophy. In her confrontation with the cynical Harthouse, she exemplifies Dickens' thesis that a good person can overcome evil with just the power of his goodness.

M'CHOAKUMCHILD

Schoolmaster in Gradgrind's school in Coketown. Well-trained in the state teacher-education factory in everything from orthography to land surveying, his only approach to education is to fill the children with nothing but hard facts. In him Dickens levels another one of his many attacks on the faults in contemporary education.

MRS. PEGLER

An old woman who first appears nameless lurking about Bounderby's house. She evinces great admiration for him and his works. She turns out to be the mother he had pensioned off and disowned.

RACHAEL

A working woman of thirty-five, with beautiful dark eyes and dark hair, who has long been in love with Stephen Blackpool. She is a sort of guardian angel to Stephen, tending his drunken wife, stopping her from drinking poison, and generally consoling him in his despair. Their relationship, tender though platonic, was thought well-described by contemporary readers.

SLACKBRIDGE

Union organizer among the Coketown mill workers, he is "an ill-made, high-shouldered man, with lowering brows, and his features crushed into a habitually sour expression. ..." With windy rhetoric he turns the workers against Stephen when he refuses to join the union. In him Dickens condemns the misuse of the workers' need and desire for unions by demagogues.

SLEARY

Proprietor of Sleary's Horseriding, a traveling circus. A stout man "with one fixed eye, and one loose eye, a voice ... like the efforts of a broken pair of bellows, a flabby surface, and a muddled head which was never sober and never drunk." He talks in an asthmatic lisp and proclaims the philosophy that people must have fun and not learn and work all the time, the antithesis to Gradgrindism. At the end he is instrumental in saving Tom from prison by slipping him out of the country right under the nose of the pursuing Bitzer.

MRS. SPARSIT

Widowed housekeeper of Mr. Bounderby, she prides herself on her lofty family connections and former opulent life. She secretly despises her vulgar employer, pities him ostentatiously when he marries Louisa, and unwittingly unmasks him by finding out his mother. She is described as a stately woman with piercing eyes under black eyebrows and a Coriolanian nose. She is "nosy," and her snooping and meddling precipitate a number of crises in the novel.

HARD TIMES

CRITICAL COMMENTARY

Hard Times was first published as a weekly serial in *Household Words*, Dickens' own magazine, from April 1 to August 12, 1854. By the tenth weekly installment the circulation of the periodical had been doubled, and, according to Edgar Johnson in *Charles Dickens: His Tragedy and Triumph* (II, 797), by the end of the serial the sales had increased four- or even five-fold. Remarkable for Dickens was that the entire book, a work of some 100,000 words, had been written in a little over five months. He complained often during its composition, writing to Forster, his friend and first biographer, "I am three parts mad, and the fourth delirious, with perpetual rushing at *Hard Times*."

The fact that he restricted himself to a short novel, written over a short period of time and to appear in twenty weekly parts, accounts for the unique structure of *Hard Times* among his novels. In most of his other works he allowed himself great elbow room. Twenty installments of about three chapters per month, his usual length, permitted the leisurely unfolding of a panoramic novel, crowded with dozens, if not hundreds of characters, and convoluted with an intricate, multiple-leveled plot. *David Copperfield*, whose writing and publishing took about two years, runs to over 850 pages in most editions.

It is true, however, that two other novels had also been published in weekly, rather than monthly, parts. *The Old Curiosity Shop* had run from April 25, 1840 to January, 1841, but it was 521 pages long in a hardbound edition. *Barnaby Rudge*, another weekly serial (from February 13, 1841, to November 27, 1841), ran to 646 pages in a hardbound edition. In contrast, *Hard Times*, in most editions runs to little more than 260 pages. As a result it has a tautness of structure and an economy of words not found in any other of Dickens' works. But precisely because it is so un-Dickensian, it is also the least popular of the major novels of Dickens.

EARLY RECEPTION

George H. Ford in *Dickens and His Readers* (1955) tells the story of its varied reception among contemporary readers. Thus one, Thomas Babington Macaulay, the well-known historian, confided to his journal on August 12, 1854, of *Hard Times*, "One excessively touching, heart-breaking passage and the rest sullen Socialism. The evils which he attacks he caricatures grossly, and with little humor." A review in Blackwood's found fault with *Hard Times* because it expressed a "petulant theory" and was too **didactic**. An American reviewer some years later, E. P. Whipple, writing in the *Atlantic Monthly* (XXXIX, 1877), states that the readers of Dickens were "vexed with an author who deviated from the course of amusing them. ..." He added the curious corollary that Dickens failed because "it is as intellectually discreditable for an educated person to engage in a crusade against the established laws of political economy as in a crusade against the established laws of the physical universe." In other words, Gradgrind is right. These critics do not account for the large sales of *Hard Times* during its first publication period. Dickens must have been doing something right.

Thomas Carlyle, the crusty Scots philosopher and critic to whom Dickens dedicated *Hard Times*, was pleased with it although he had a general contempt for novels. It was he who urged Dickens to attack the "vast blockheadism" of Victorian England, and who had fired Dickens with the view that industrialism is a soul-killing evil.

John Ruskin another Victorian prophet and critic, found in Dickens' *Hard Times* a useful ally in his battle against industrialized ugliness in architecture and life. In "A Note on *Hard Times*," which appeared in the *Cornhill Magazine* (II, 1860), he urged that the novel "be studied with close and earnest care by persons interested in social questions." The novel, he states, "is with many persons seriously diminished because Mr. Bounderby is a dramatic monster, instead of a characteristic example of a worldly master; and Stephen Blackpool a dramatic perfection, instead of a characteristic example of an honest workman." Still, it is probably "the greatest he has written."

LATE NINETEENTH CENTURY

As the century continued, opinions of *Hard Times* also continued to fluctuate. Professor George Saintsbury, writing on *Dickens in the Cambridge History of English Literature*, put *Hard Times* only above *Our Mutual Friend* as the worst of the novels. Yet Margaret Oliphant in *The Victorian Age of English Literature* (1892) wrote that *Hard Times* "contains in the **episodes** of Stephen and Rachael one of the best pieces of serious writing which Dickens ever did." This emphasis on its seriousness was to be repeated by subsequent critics, sometimes as the only redeeming feature of the novel.

SHAW

George Bernard Shaw, the Irish playwright, critic, and one-time Socialist, wrote an introduction to the Waverly edition of *Hard Times* (1912). He finds it a serious novel, although belittled by the *Encyclopedia Britannica* editors. "*Hard Times* was written to make you uncomfortable; and it will make you uncomfortable (and serve you right) though it will perhaps interest you more and certainly leave a deeper scar on you, than any two of its predecessors."

Shaw finds that the book suffers from the "extravagantly ridiculous speeches" put into the mouths of Mrs. Sparsit, Sissy, and Louisa. A real failure in the book, he finds, is Slackbridge, the union organizer, who "is a mere figment of the middle-class imagination." He is implausible, for "no such man would be listened to by a meeting of English factory hands." Shaw feels that Dickens was simply out of his element in portraying industrial workers.

BAKER

Ernest A. Baker, writing of *Hard Times* in his monumental *History of the English Novel*, 1936 (VII, 297–99), finds that it is but "little representative of Dickens ... beyond the sincerity and ardor with which he champions the unfortunates bleeding under the wheels of modern industrialism." But even here, "there is prejudice in his statement of the case; the conclusion is forestalled from the beginning." Baker finds the story of Stephen and Rachael "pathos and nothing but pathos." Only "by sheer force and indignation, Dickens galvanized his two personifications of blind slave-driving energy and greed, Gradgrind and Bounderby, into a semblance of life." The novel must be considered a failure although it "has now become a chapter, or at least a famous page, in the annals of social controversy."

HOUSE

Humphry House, in The *Dickens World* (1941), calls *Hard Times* "the least read of the novels and probably also the least enjoyed by those who do read it." He reiterates the attitude of G. B. Shaw that "Dickens was writing of people and things quite outside the range of his own experience." House points out that in the 'fifties Dickens began using his novels "as a vehicle of more concentrated sociological argument," and that *Hard Times* in particular "is one of Dickens' most thought-about books." In this novel the ideas were too hazily conceived to animate the plot. For one thing Dickens did not understand the true nature of employer-employee relations in a complex industrial society. He did not draw from the experiences of Stephen Blackpool the proper inference that an individual worker does not have much bargaining power. Dickens still felt that man-to-man benevolence can solve the class struggle. The result is that *Hard Times* pleased neither the radical reformers nor the conservatives. As House concludes, "The book is ultimately unsatisfying and oddly uncomfortable to nearly all its readers."

Hard Times continued to languish in critical esteem into more recent times. Edward Wagenknecht, who devotes a whole chapter to Dickens in *The Cavalcade of the English Novel*, has little more to say of *Hard Times* except that it "is Dickens' most arid book." Walter Allen, whose *The English Novel* (1955) is among the most recent histories of the **genre**, merely lists the title among the social novels of Dickens.

LEAVIS

It is F. R. Leavis in *The Great Tradition* (1948) who makes the strongest attempt to rehabilitate the novel in modern critical esteem. He begins by not even including Dickens among the English novelists in "the great tradition." Dickens is only a great entertainer, like Sir Walter Scott. He writes, "The adult mind doesn't as a rule find in Dickens the challenge to an unusual and sustained seriousness." Only *Hard Times* is an exception and for this reason has "escaped recognition for the great thing it is."

Thus Leavis praises *Hard Times* for the very reason earlier critics deplored, namely that it is an un-Dickensian novel. He feels that because Dickens was "too urgently possessed by his themes," he desisted from his "usual repetitive overdoing and loose inclusiveness." Leavis considers *Hard Times* nearly perfect: "The fable is perfect; the symbolic and representative values are inevitable, and, sufficiently plain at once, yield fresh subtleties as the action develops naturally in its convincing historical way."

Leavis considers that the novel's main **theme**, "the confutation of Utilitarianism by life," is done "with great subtlety." The characters, in their symbolic function, are well done. Thus Sissy represents "vitality as well as goodness." She is "generous, impulsive life … the antithesis of calculating self-interest." She is contrasted with Bitzer, "the thin-blooded, quasi-mechanical product of Gradgrindery. "

Sleary's Horseriding, out of which Sissy comes, is also a symbol. It is "human kindness ... associated with vitality." The circus people, "representing human spontaneity," possess at the same time "highly developed skills ... that bring poise, pride, and confident ease. ..." Although "their skills have no values for the Utilitarian calculus," ... "they minister to vital human needs." They bring the imagination-starved factory hands of Coketown amusement, art, and "the spectacle of triumphant activity."

JOHNSON

Perhaps it would be appropriate to let Edgar Johnson, whose *Charles Dickens: His Tragedy and Triumph* (1952) promises to be the definitive study, have the last word. He deplores the tendency of commentators "to ignore or belittle the dark masterpieces of Dickens' maturity because they will not let us close our eyes on the clamorous problems that threaten us with disaster." *Hard Times*, according to Johnson, "is a morality drama, stark, formalized, allegorical, dominated by the mood of piercing through to the underlying meaning of the industrial scene rather than describing it in minute detail." Coketown could be Birmingham or Leeds, or even Pittsburgh. What could stand against the "cruelty of mine and mill ... against the bleak utilitarian philosophy with which they were allied ... except the flowering of the humane imagination and the ennoblement of the heart?"

As long as the problems of industrial ugliness, of the monotony of factory labor, of exploitation of labor by management, or of the coercion of labor by unions exist, *Hard Times* will have something to say to us. The depressing thing about the novel is not its tone of utter seriousness, its lack of Dickensian humor, but the fact that the problems which he wrote about over a century ago are still very much with us. The counterparts of Gradgrind, of Bounderby, of M'Choakumchild, and of Bitzer are among us today and we all recognize some of them. This is what makes *Hard Times* a great, universal novel, worth reading and close study.

HARD TIMES

ESSAY QUESTIONS AND ANSWERS

Question: What is the main plot of *Hard Times*?

Answer: There is considerable dispute about this. Earlier critics thought that the affairs of Stephen Blackpool and Rachael provided the main plot thread. The troubles of Stephen with his alcoholic wife, his inability to divorce her and marry Rachael, whom he loves, his refusal to join the union, his ostracism by the workers at the instigation of the union leader, his firing by Bounderby, his unjustly being accused of robbery, his death on the way back to clear himself - all these events certainly are the elements of plot. But that this is the main plot, is doubtful. Stephen does not even appear until Chapter 10, and plays the main part in only five or six later chapters.

Another view is that Louisa and her life provide the main plot thread. We meet her first peeping in at Sleary's circus. We are given glimpses of her cold, loveless home life, her dutiful but sullen relation to her father, her perfunctory relation to her mother. We learn of her distaste for Bounderby and her affection for her brother Tom, who so little deserves it. We see her married to Bounderby after a session with her father in which her inner rebellion almost flares out. We follow her loveless marriage to an almost adulterous affair with Harthouse. Finally we see her marriage and her composure break down completely. In one sense *Hard Times* is thus the case history of a typical middle-class "arranged" marriage, based on all considerations except love and compatibility.

A third view is that the conversion or redemption of Gradgrind, the breakdown of his philosophic system compounded of utilitarian "facts" and self-interest, is the main plot. Of all the characters in the novel, Gradgrind is the least static and undergoes the greatest change. The behavior of the others is predictable, their development a foregone conclusion. As a character study, the sorrowful education of Gradgrind to a renewed humaneness is well done and plausible. But it does not occupy the amount of space to make it the main plotline of the novel in itself.

Question: What is the structure of *Hard times*?

Answer: *Hard Times* is unique among Dickens' novels for its taut structure, its brevity, and its general economy of words. It is divided into three books: "Sowing," Reaping," and "Garnering." The terms, taken from agriculture, refer to the philosophy of Gradgrindism, applying to it the Biblical saying, "As ye sow, so ye shall reap." We see it sowed in the fallow minds of the schoolchildren at Gradgrind's school, and in the children of Gradgrind himself. We see the seeds take root in Louisa and Tom Gradgrind, and in Bitzer. We see the philosophy in full bloom in Bounderby and Gradgrind. At the end of Book 1 the system is apparently triumphant.

In the second book we see the reaping of the effects of the philosophy. The unhappiness of Louisa's marriage, the selfishness, profligacy, and dishonesty of Tom, the calculating self-interest of Bitzer are all its results. In a way, the ostracism of Stephen by the union men is dictated by Gradgrindian self-interest too, as is Stephen's firing by Bounderby. At the end of Book 2, with Stephen's disappearance, Tom's dishonesty, and Louisa's return home from her broken marriage, the system has broken down into failure. Its effects have been reaped.

The third book, "Garnering," merely picks up the broken pieces ("to garner" means to pick up the cut grain). Just as cut grain is no longer living, so the picked-up pieces of Gradgrindism are dead or at least negative. Stephen dies, Bounderby is exposed as a fraud, Tom as a thief, Louisa's marriage is beyond mending, and Gradgrind has lost his socio-political faith. All that has been garnered is death, defeat, and disaster.

It is interesting to note that the spatial relationship among the three books corresponds to their agricultural titles. Sowing, a lengthy process in farming, takes sixteen chapters; Reaping, less time-consuming, takes twelve; and Garnering, the shortest process, takes only nine chapters.

Question: What symbolism is used in *Hard Times*?

Answer: Critics have long noted that Dickens made an increasing use of symbols in his novels as he developed. In *Hard Times* they are not too frequent, but they are effectively used. Among his symbols are the serpent-like smoke plumes from the factory chimneys, mentioned on at least six occasions. The Coketown sky is never free of them, the poisonous, pollutant effects of industry which endlessly coil over it. Similarly significant are the steam engines of the factories which are always described as "melancholy mad elephants" in their monotonous motions.

These are indicative of the maddening, brainless monotony of industrial work.

Another symbol, one connected exclusively with Louisa, is that of a fire. She is often seen gazing at the dying embers of a fire. It symbolizes the feeble glow of the imagination still left in her. It dies when she agrees to marry Bounderby.

There are a host of minor symbols and images as well: the squareness of everything connected with Gradgrind, the multiple wind references in connection with Bounderby. Sleary's circus is, in a way, also a symbol. It stands for the life of spontaneity, amusement, and art - the antithesis of utilitarianism.

Question: What does Sissy Jupe represent in the novel?

Answer: Sissy Jupe, the daughter of the broken-down circus performer who deserts her, is a sort of catalytic agent in *Hard Times*. Just as a catalytic agent is the thing which precipitates a chemical reaction, but itself remains unchanged, so in *Hard Times* Sissy Jupe affects the lives of others, but is unchanged.

We first meet her at the school, threatening the very existence of its arid educational system by defending imagination against facts. When Gradgrind wants to expel her for this, her father's desertion forces Gradgrind to keep her on. His taking her into his household, a weak moment of compassion for him, is to change his life although he does not realize it. This small act of humanity leads to his eventual redemption. It is Sissy who fans the latent rebellion of Louisa, who brings happiness to the younger Gradgrind children, who persuades the cynical Harthouse to give up his pursuit of Louisa. It is she who saves Tom from prison by hiding him at the circus.

Actually, outside of her brief appearances in these crucial scenes, we know little of her. She is a sort of good fairy, spreading sunshine and infecting others with her virtue. If *Hard Times* had been the typical Dickens long novel. Sissy might have been developed into an Agnes of *David Copperfield*, the Victorian male's ideal of "the angel in the house."

Question: What are some of the evils attacked in *Hard Times*?

Answer: As in all of his novels, Dickens in *Hard Times* lays siege to a number of social abuses. Primary is what he calls Gradgrindism, the justification for cold, calculating exploitation of the working class by a philosophic system which rationalized it in the name of supposedly scientific laws of political economy. Of course Dickens oversimplifies. Gradgrindism combines elements from Malthus' *Essay on Population* (1798), Adam Smith's The Wealth of Nations (1776), and the works of Jeremy Bentham, the apostle of utilitarianism. It is significant in this regard that two of the small children of Gradgrind are named Adam Smith Gradgrind and Malthus Gradgrind.

Another abuse under attack is the rigidity of British divorce laws. As in Roman Catholic countries, in Anglican England divorce was not possible, but a marriage could be dissolved by an Act of Parliament. This was a long-drawn-out and very expensive procedure, open only to the wealthy and well connected. Dickens, himself on the brink of separation from an incompatible wife, had personal reasons for his bitterness toward the unjust marriage laws. In portraying the agony of Stephen's catastrophic marriage, he mirrors his own frustrations.

Bad education, as in so many of his other novels, also comes under attack in *Hard Times*. The school of Gradgrind is bad because it stifles the imagination. It supposes that facts are knowledge, that statistics and definitions will make for wisdom. Dickens modeled the opening scene in the classroom, with its stultifying questions, on an actual examination by the National Teachers' Board. He sneers at teachers' training methods, writing that if they learned fewer abstruse subjects, they would be able to teach better. As in his other attacks on education, while he points to real defects, he offers no constructive criticism, no better alternative.

Question: What part does color **imagery** play in *Hard Times*?

Answer: Besides symbols, colors play a large part in *Hard Times*, especially black and white. Sissy Jupe, who personifies life and goodness, is dark-haired, dark-eyed, and suffused with color from the s n. Bitzer, her opposite, who personifies the evils to which the philosophy of calculated self-interest leads, is light-haired, light-eyed, pale, as if all color had been drained from him. After Sissy lives with the Gradgrinds a while she too develops a pale, waxen complexion. This is contrary to usual symbolic values in which white represents good and black stands for evil.

Black is also in the name of the unfortunate good worker, Stephen Blackpool. Rachael, the angelic working woman whom he loves, also has black hair and eyes. Of course this symbolism can be carried too far. Mrs. Sparsit, the meddling evil genie of Mr. Bounderby, also has black eyes and eyebrows. The houses of Coketown are of red brick, blackened by coal soot. But in general Dickens in *Hard Times* equates dark colors with good and light colors with evil.

BIBLIOGRAPHY AND GUIDE TO FURTHER RESEARCH

BOOKS

Allen, Walter. *The English Novel.* New York, 1955.

Baker, Ernest A. *The History of the English Novel.* 10 vols.; Vol. VII, "The Age of Dickens and Thackeray." New York, 1936.

Butt, John, and Kathleen Tillotson. *Dickens at Work.* London, 1957.

Chancellor, E. Bereford. *Dickens and His Times.* London, 1937.

Chesterton, Gilbert Keith. *Charles Dickens: A Critical Study.* New York, 1913.

Cruikshank, Robert J. *Charles Dickens and Early Victorian, England.* London, 1949.

Ford, George H. *Dickens and His Readers.* Princeton, 1955. Paperback.

House, Humphry. *The Dickens World.* London, 1941. Paperback.

Jackson, T. A. *Charles Dickens: The Progress of a Radical.* London, 1938.

Johnson, Edgar. *Charles Dickens: His Tragedy and Triumph*, 2 vols. New York, 1952.

Leavis, F. R. *"Hard Times: An Analytic Note," The Great Tradition*. London, 1948. Paperback.

Miller, J. Hillis. *Charles Dickens: The World of His Novels*. Cambridge, Mass., 1958.

Maurois, Andre. *Dickens*. New York, 1935.

Orwell, George. *Dickens, Dali, and Others*. New York, 1946. Paperback.

Pearson, Hesketh. *Dickens: His Character, Comedy, and Career*. New York, 1949.

Pope-Hennessey, Una. *Charles Dickens*. London, 1946.

Shaw, George Bernard. *"Introduction," Hard Times* (Waverly Edition). London, 1912.

Symons, Julian. *Charles Dickens*. New York, 1951.

Wagenknecht, Edward. *Cavalcade of the English Novel*, 2nd ed. New York, 1954.

_____. *The Man Charles Dickens*. New York, 1929.

Watt, William W. *"Introduction," Hard Times* (Rinehart Edition). New York, 1958. Paperback.

Wilson, Edmund. "Dickens: The Two Scrooges," *The Wound and the Bow*. New York, 1947.

ARTICLES

Christian, Mildred G. "Carlyle's Influence upon the Social Theory of Dickens," *The Trollopian*, no. 4, I (1947), 27–35 and II (1947), 11–26.

Grubb, Gerald. "Dickens' Pattern of Weekly Serialization," *English Literary History*, IX (1942), 141–156.

Waldock, A. J. A. "*The Status of Hard Times*," *Southerly*, IX (1948), 33–39.

Stevenson, Lionel. "Dickens' Dark Novels, 1851–1857," *Sewanee Review*, LI (1943), 398–409.

FURTHER ARTICLES ON HARD TIMES

For additional material on particular problems in *Hard Times* the student is referred to the following scholarly periodicals:

The Dickensian, a quarterly published in London by the Dickens Fellowship.

Nineteenth Century Fiction (formerly The Trollopian).

Publication of the Modern Language Association (PMLA).

Victorian Newsletter.

Victorian Studies.

SUGGESTIONS FOR RESEARCH PAPER TOPICS

Hard Times and mid-Victorian England

The influence of Thomas Carlyle on *Hard Times*

Hard Times and economic theories

Hard Times as an attack on utilitarianism

Capital vs. Labor in *Hard Times*

Dickens' view of labor unions in *Hard Times*

Dickens' view of industrialism in *Hard Times*

Dickens' view of education in *Hard Times*

Dickens' view of marriage and divorce in *Hard Times*

Dickens' view of religion in *Hard Times*

Dickens as a social critic in *Hard Times*

The structure of *Hard Times*

Hard Times as a morality play

The "wasteland" landscape of *Hard Times*

The symbols and **imagery** of *Hard Times*

The effect of weekly serialization on *Hard Times*

The reception of *Hard Times* by contemporaries

EXPLORE THE ENTIRE LIBRARY OF BRIGHT NOTES STUDY GUIDES

From Shakespeare to Sinclair Lewis and from Plato to Pearl S. Buck, The Bright Notes Study Guide library spans hundreds of volumes, providing clear and comprehensive insights into the world's greatest literature. Discover more, faster with the Bright Notes Study Guide to the classics you're reading today.

See the entire library of available Bright Notes guides at **BrightNotes.com**

Available in print and digital wherever books are sold

IP INFLUENCE PUBLISHERS

Lightning Source UK Ltd.
Milton Keynes UK
UKHW021409161121
394066UK00008B/450